D1498767

The Challenge of Being Single

by
Marie Edwards
& Eleanor Hoover

PUBLISHED BY J.P. TARCHER, INC., LOS ANGELES

Distributed by Hawthorn Books, Inc., New York

TO SINGLE MEN AND WOMEN EVERYWHERE

Library of Congress Catalog Card Number: 73-92096

ISBN: 0-87477-020-3

Published by J.P. Tarcher, Inc.
9110 Sunset Blvd., Los Angeles, Calif. 90069

Printed in the United States of America

Published simultaneously in Canada by
Prentice-Hall of Canada, Ltd.
1870 Birchmont Road, Scarborough, Ontario

1 2 3 4 5 6 7 8 9

PREFACE

This book grew out of many years of working as a psychologist, with both singles and marrieds, particularly in personal growth and encounter groups. During that time, I gradually became aware that in a variety of ways singles felt stigmatized—even ostracized—solely because they were not married. The biggest surprise was that many of them were not aware that other singles felt that way too.

An odd aspect of second-class citizenship is that unless someone points it out to you or you point it out to yourself, you can go through life suffering in silence various indignities, external or self-imposed, without realizing that you are surrounded by perhaps millions of others who feel exactly as you do. It has been the habit of most singles not to even admit to themselves how they felt, much less express their feelings to others. Each assumed that he or she was suffering all alone.

Being single presented such a challenge to so many people that I wondered what would happen if I offered a course called "The Challenge of Being Single" in a university setting where I could obtain additional data that would uncover the "truth" about singles—their feelings, attitudes, behavior, and ideas. Having been divorced after eleven years of marriage and having been a single parent as well, raising my son alone from the age of nine, I remember vividly many of the vexing problems, experiences, and frustrations of the single life.

At this time the University of Southern California was seeking to extend its work in the humanities in its continuing education division. After reviewing my course proposal, they invited me to follow through on it, and for four years I have continued to conduct "Challenge of Being Single" workshops there and on many other campuses, gathering information on the single life.

Single men and women of all ages, eighteen through seventy-two, come to "Challenge of Being Single" workshops, with the largest number in their twenties, thirties, and forties. Sometimes a few married people enroll too, mostly to see what single life is all about prior to possible reentry.

Originally the workshops were held over a ten-week period, but in order to intensify the work and accelerate the development of feelings of closeness and kinship, the format was changed to a two-day weekend from 10 A.M. to 6 P.M. on both Saturday and Sunday. Group size ranges from sixty to one hundred participants. For greater ease of discussion the group later divides into groups of six to ten to work on specific problems and to examine various solutions, expectations, and feelings about single life. Typically, on each of the two days there is a morning and afternoon lecture emphasizing the many positive and challenging aspects of singlehood and summarizing the information and ideas gleaned from working with singles.

This book, then, is the distillation of those years of research and in-depth interviews with several thousand single men and women—divorced, widowed, separated, and never-married—and, of course, of my own personal feelings. It's "how-to's" are not armchair theorizing, but come from pragmatic study of real-life singles, particularly those who manage their lives most successfully.

I was also curious about singles other than those in my "Challenge" workshops and wondered whether they felt similarly about their singlehood. The fact that innumerable singles shared the same attitudes emerged when stories about the course began appearing in newspapers across the country and letters came to me which reflected these feelings as well as a new-found self-image and pride. These letters contained such comments as:

> At last someone is speaking for the neglected singles. I'm sick of always being asked, "Why isn't a nice person like you married?" Tell them out there I don't want to be married!

> I'm single. I'm not irresponsible, frigid, a man-hater, or a two-headed monster; I'm tired of people thinking I must be at least one of these or else I'd be married!

> I'm twenty-four and I really don't want to be married. Not now, anyway. How can I get my parents off my back? They keep trying to push me into marriage every time I go out with a new person!

> I've been divorced now for five years after being married for twenty and I love my single life. I feel so free! I don't think I ever want to get married again.

The letters all made the same strong point: Many singles are tired of society's negative image and are more determined than ever not to be pushed into marriage.

However they feel about marriage when they come to the

workshop—and certainly many singles would say that they still want to get married, sometime—marriage itself is not very high on the personal agendas of most of the participants. At the workshop they discover that they are not alone, that many other singles feel the same way they do, that many are coping quite successfully with problems similar to theirs. They trade solutions, experiences, ideas. When they come in, they say, "I didn't know so many others feel the way I do"; when they leave, it is often with the feeling that "It really is okay to be single."

Many also make significant discoveries about themselves as they relate to other people. They find out they like each other and in ways they never would have predicted. While they often come, initially, to meet "datable" people, they leave with something more valuable: a sense of empathy with everyone there. At the outset, most of the divorced say they prefer talking to the divorced, the never-married to the never-married, the young to the young, the older to the older—but it doesn't stay that way. Before long, almost everyone is talking in mixed groups. They leave with a whole new sense of confidence about themselves and a new positive outlook on their own singlehood.

Because there have been so many myths and so much misinformation about singles, and so little about how singles really feel about themselves, I felt a book needed to be written. When I decided to put my ideas on paper, I asked Eleanor Hoover, a well-known writer in the field of psychology and a correspondent with *Time* magazine, and also a psychologist, to lend her writing skills and professional insights. This book is the result of that collaboration.

Marie Babare Edwards
Los Angeles, California
January 2, 1974

ACKNOWLEDGMENTS

We wish to express our gratitude to Jeremy Tarcher, our publisher, for his excellent ideas and suggestions and for his masterful diplomacy and understanding in seeing us through the challenge and excitement of writing this book; to Jim Miller, our editor, for his enriching ideas and careful editing, and to Theron Raines, our agent, who had faith in our concept of singles.

We are also indebted to Dean Paul Hadley, Dean Roy Adamson, Dr. James Peterson, Dr. Clinton Phillips, Dr. Calfred Broderick, William Campbell, John Stoner, and Ellen Dahlgren of the University of Southern California for their encouraging and continuing interest in the "Challenge of Being Single" programs.

Similarly, we are grateful to the University of California and its divisions of continuing education, as well as many other colleges and universities for their continued support.

We should also like to express our thanks to Drs. George Lehner and Bernauer Newton, friends and teachers extraordinary, for their faith in one particular single; to Betty Idell and Mary Ann Hammer, for their great patience and good humor in typing the many versions of the manuscript; and to all those across the country who wrote so many encouraging letters in support of the singles movement—and, of course, our deepest thanks to all participants in the "Challenge" workshops, whose ideas, cooperation, enthusiasm, and perceptive insights made this book possible.

TABLE OF CONTENTS

Preface

It's Okay to Be Single — An Introduction

If you are one of the 43 million singles in this country, you are undoubtedly—and painfully—aware of the considerable difficulties of being happily single in a society where being paired is widely regarded as the only natural, sane, healthy, and proper way to be. Daily you are reminded in a dozen little ways—and some not so little—that you are out of step.

It doesn't matter whether you are a man or a woman, divorced, widowed, separated, or never-married; if you are not paired, you invite—and receive—a wide variety of overt and covert prejudices, slights, misinterpretations, and out-right discriminations. And this shows up not only in society's negative attitudes, which are certainly widespread, but also in bold assaults on your pocketbook and livelihood. As a single, you know all too well that you pay higher income taxes and often find difficulty in getting credit, insurance, loans, job promotions—even decent seating in a good restaurant.

Most books and articles about the single life ignore these problems and concentrate on instructing the single in how to get through the trying period of singlehood with the least fuss and trouble. Their basic assumption is that you *must* want to get married, and the sooner you do so the better. Meanwhile you are just biding your time until a magical "other" steps forth to correct and complete the miserable half-state in which you are supposed to exist.

This book challenges these assumptions. It is a positive book about the singles' world, and it proposes a revolutionary change in attitude about the single life.

It does not ignore the many disadvantages of being single in a couples' world, nor does it present the unrealistic view that being single is the best of all possible life-styles for everyone. It is certainly not against marriage. But its basic assumption is that you should have a clear, unfettered choice about whether or not to marry without facing disapproval if you do choose singlehood as a way of life.

And heretical though it may seem to a paired world, there are many healthy, well-adjusted singles who do not want to get married—ever. They are already so actively enjoying their lives that they definitely prefer to remain as they are. They refuse to let society's pressure to pair force them out of a life they find so rewarding. They have found—and this is a major thesis of this book—that it is indeed *okay to be single*. And for some it is more than okay; it is a superior way of life.

The early chapters of this book are concerned with exploring the many myths and discriminations that plague all singles as well as the special problems of the divorced, separated, never-married, and widowed. We strongly believe that before you can begin to change your life, you must first accept the reality of the way things are.

Dealing with loneliness, one of the greatest problems of

single life, is discussed, we trust, in a helpful way in Chapter 4. In other chapters we look at going out alone, meeting other singles, love and sex, and the other major aspects of the single life. We have also included chapters which we frankly hope will inspire you. One is on the importance of friends and there is one on the greatest advantage of being single— freedom.

Many of these chapters are only starting points. Dozens, and in some cases, even hundreds, of books have been written about some of these topics. A subject-by-subject suggested reading list derived in part from recommendations people have made in "Challege" workshops has been included in the back of this book.

Some of the books on this list contain ideas directly contradictory to those in other books on the list. That doesn't matter. We are not claiming that any one of them contains the ultimate truth, for in human affairs there are almost as many ways of finding fulfillment as there are individuals seeking it.

Each of these books has, however, passed the test of providing many readers with counsel that proved to be important to them. Since we have tried in this book to relate the single life to certain topics, rather than to cover the topics in their entirety, these books can greatly deepen your understanding of the world and yourself.

We very strongly urge that you get and use these books to build yourself a library to which you can frequently return for advice and wisdom. You may discover them to be friends of great value.

This book concludes with a Singles Manifesto that we hope will be the opening salvo in a singles liberation (or is it celebration?) movement.

The Challenge of Being Single is intended to dramatically

improve the quality of your life. It is for those of you who know—or have begun to suspect—that the direction of life should not be left to blind chance nor determined by equally blind tradition. It is for those of you who wonder how other singles cope with the special problems and frustrations of being single.

It provides answers and solutions that have worked for other singles. It suggests new directions for a more satisfying life, whether you want to stay single or become part of a pair. But it does more than that really—it challenges you to realistically appraise where you are in your life and where you want to be. We hope that you will find it a book full of solid, practical advice, which will help you develop the positive attitude about single life that is necessary before you can take full advantage of it.

If, occasionally, you feel that we are overstating our case, it is perhaps because we are trying to counteract generations of conventional thinking about singlehood. It is not always easy to fight through to a common ground. New ideas are seldom easy to present—and ours may even qualify as evangelical. But we can hardly do less.

Like other changing social institutions, marriage went quietly about its business for many centuries until it started to groan and creak of some built-in contradictions of its own. Then someone had to say that maybe we should rethink what marriage is basically about and whether it should be the sole way of structuring personal lives. Today, we are saying it is time to rethink what being single is all about. It is an idea whose time has come.

We have lock-stepped through history so long in a Noah's Ark lineup of twosomes that it may be difficult to grasp that one of the emergent, really liberating ideas of our time may well be the final lifting of singlehood from a weary waiting ground for marriage to a new status as a thoroughly viable, rewarding, enjoyable, creative, and satisfying alternative to marriage.

1. "How Come You're Not Married?"

Linda, a pretty twenty-five-year-old graduate history student, works part-time and has never married—although she has come close twice. When most of her school friends married, Linda felt no similar compulsion, neither from friends' subtle pressures nor from the more direct pressures of her parents. She loved her work and school, and she enjoyed her freedom. Yet in her day-to-day life, she began to be uneasy. She felt uncomfortable whenever the subject of marriage arose or when someone would ask the ungracious question, "Why aren't you married?" Indeed, why wasn't she? Her troubling conclusion was that she should have been married long ago. Everybody thought so. Something must be wrong with her.

Then when her younger sister started making wedding plans, Linda found she couldn't eat and had trouble sleeping. She consulted a doctor and was told she was developing an ulcer. Finally Linda forced herself to examine her real feelings about marriage and her own future.

Always before, she put off facing these questions with the thought that she would get married "someday, when the right man came along." She now discovered, to her surprise, that there was another, more satisfying answer to that recurring question, "How come you're not married?" She could honestly say that she didn't want to get married now—perhaps not ever. She preferred to pursue her education and career.

It was so simple—but never before had she been able to even consider the possibility that she really didn't wish to be married. Unconsciously she had felt that to acknowledge this would have confirmed to herself and to the world at large that she was selfish, unfeminine, cold, unemotional, or simply incomplete as a person. When Linda accepted her true feelings about marriage, many of her tensions disappeared, and now she confronts her single life in a positive way.

Norm, a fifty-year-old widower, doesn't escape the pressure to get married either. Although his wife died only a year ago, his friends (married, of course) are relentless in their efforts to find a new wife for him. Not once, but many times they have told him, "It's just not natural for you to live alone. You need someone to look after you." They continually invite him to dinner, pairing him up with a distant cousin, a new co-worker, or a neighbor down the street.

Norm's income is adequate. He likes his work, and he is beginning to like his new freedom to come and go as he pleases, to make decisions without consulting anyone. Generally, he is finding life much more pleasant than he thought possible.

So when the pressure-to-pair from his well-meaning friends finally became too much, he said, "Look, I appreciate your wanting to help me, but I don't want to get married again. Not now, anyway. My life isn't all roses, but I'm discovering a lot of advantages in being single. So please lay off this pairing game. I want to be free. You're married and you may not understand, but it really feels good to be on my own."

It may be that Linda's and Norm's reactions to being single are not typical of most singles. The majority of single women marry before they reach 24, and the majority of widowers and divorced people remarry, too, but Linda and Norm do represent a relatively new phenomenon—the increasingly large number of single persons who could easily marry if they wanted to but are choosing to remain unmarried.

They are successfully single, and this is a book about them and about other singles and how they live their lives. The challenge of being single is even greater for those who want to get married but are not, and this book will also introduce concepts and techniques for making their single life as potentially fulfilling and complete as they have always dreamed that married life would be.

SOCIETY'S THEME SONG: "WHAT'S WRONG WITH YOU?"

Linda and Norm, like most singles (even those whose recent divorces indicate something of their feeling about marriage) spend a good deal of time explaining to other people why they are not married. Women have to do more of this, but men, although they have more freedom than women, are still under subtle, continuing pressure from friends, family, and co-workers to get married: a pressure aptly summed up by the cliché, "Have I got a girl for you!"

Of course, when people inquire, "How come you're not married?" they often say they intend it as a compliment and even phrase it, "How come a nice (or attractive or intelligent) girl or guy like you isn't married?" Nonetheless, most singles find the question embarrassing and irritating—even more so as they grow older, for the tacit assumption is that if you aren't married you suffer from some deep, dark, emotional malaise. Certainly you must be emotionally immature and unable to accept normal adult responsibility. Perhaps you're frigid, impotent, or sexually deviant. Something's wrong with you, for sure.

Novelist Rona Jaffe describes her own encounter with The Question: "Being a single career woman has had its drawbacks, but things are not as hard as they used to be. Ten years ago it was embarrassing to be single. As soon as I met a man, he would ask me how come I had never been married—in other words—'Prove that you're not a freak.' I was always tempted to say that I had spent my entire adult life in an insane asylum but, now that I was out, I would start looking."

In one "Challenge" workshop a single woman put it this way: "When I meet a single man I always ask myself, 'What's wrong with him?' and I'm pretty sure he's asking himself the same thing about me. One thing we're each sure of is that something is wrong with the other one—and we suspect with ourselves, too." Is it any wonder that many singles secretly still think of themselves as something akin to Rona Jaffe's "freaks"? This social contempt eventually brings about self-contempt.

Like any group that has been constantly ignored or downgraded, singles come to believe what others say about them. And even though they may not acknowledge it consciously, they behave as if they believe it by limiting the scope of their existence, by not taking chances in their personal and work lives, by not really choosing when they have the opportunity, and by seeing themselves as only temporary people, not rooted firmly in the present.

Sometimes this self-devaluing hits singles at significant times later in life when they least expect it. Long after many singles have made peace with themselves and managed to successfully convince themselves that there were "good reasons" for not marrying in their younger years, they begin to recognize that they are getting older and that the right person isn't appearing on the scene. At that point their low self-image as a single finally emerges.

Russell, a thirty-nine-year-old high school teacher, told a "Challenge" workshop: "It was bad enough when I hit thirty, but in a month I'll be forty. Now I'm really wondering if something isn't wrong with me because I find I honestly don't want to get married. I've had some long-lasting, good relationships with women, but they always ended up wanting to get married and I didn't feel the need. Maybe if I wanted kids of my own it would be different, but I don't.

"It's not that I don't like kids, but I just don't feel the *need* to father any of my own. And if you don't want children, I think marriage is unnecessary. Besides, I have to travel a lot and could be only a part-time husband. That doesn't seem like much of a marriage to me."

The never-married, particularly, often feel that they have missed something (although they are not sure what) by remaining single—which leads to their frequent comment, "I feel so temporary," or "I have this gnawing feeling that I've somehow missed the boat and it makes me feel like only half a person."

Still, Russell, who seems to know what he wants and appears to have obtained it, nonetheless feels that he shouldn't really want it and that something is wrong because by forty "a man ought to be married." Russell can, at least, call himself a confirmed bachelor and not feel too bad. But any never-married woman of that age is considered a spinster, and that is never intended as a compliment.

IS MARRIAGE NECESSARY?

Where does this negative view of being single come from, and is it justified? Historically, marriage was essential for economic and physical survival. In earlier days there was no question about the necessity of a basic division of labor. Men tilled the soil and hunted; women helped to work the land, prepared what was brought in from harvest, and had children. Together, they formed a united front against the hazards of nature and produced as many children as possible to help with these survival tasks. Only pairing provided the teamwork necessary for the maintenance and growth of society.

In those days, indeed, marriage and family clearly met the needs in most people's lives. Today, however, in the Western world, we have a society with far different economic and social realities than have ever existed before, and there is no longer unanimity about the need for, or the ability of, marriage and childbearing to provide fulfillment for the individual or for society.

Some current social critics have even gone so far as to say that the traditional monogamous marriage is unhealthy for the development of the individual, as it "locks in" not only man and wife but also the child, allowing no one to develop fully and freely. This is admittedly an extreme point of view, but as distinguished an anthropologist as Ashley Montagu charges that the American nuclear family—a husband, wife, and one or more children—is a social unit which systematically produces mental illness in its members.

Psychologist Richard Farson also indicts the nuclear family, which in his view "can't stand for any of its members to get better." He means by this that the family can't stand for any member to improve his or her social, economic, or even personal life because it is often too unsettling to the stability of the family as a whole.

Many, perhaps most, social scientists wouldn't agree with these positions. They still feel that marriage continues to do a fairly good job of meeting basic human needs. Unquestionably in many cases it does, but in many other cases it does not, as testified to by divorce statistics in the United States and other countries of the Western world.

Another opinion about this issue is that of sociologist Jessie Bernard. In her recent book, *The Future of Marriage,* she says that every marriage consists of two marriages—his and hers. Each partner looks at the relationship from his own vantage point and expects from it basically whatever society has told him he should expect. Marriage, Dr. Bernard concludes, is generally good for men because they expect care, comfort, and ordered domesticity, and usually get it. But it is hazardous for women because their needs for self-identity are frequently not met in the home. Marriage therefore, she believes, literally makes thousands of women sick.

Still, Dr. Bernard thinks that marriage has a future, and she feels that "men and women will continue to want to celebrate their mutuality, will continue to want intimacy, and will continue to want to experience that mystic unity. . . ." But she sees marriage of the future as different from the rather uniform institution it has been in the past. She feels, and we agree, that it may no longer be a lifetime contract, or even involve the sharing of one household. It may disavow parenthood while pledging an even deeper commitment between partners than it does now. It will certainly, if it is to survive, recognize the autonomy of women and their need for greater economic independence.

Other scientists are also questioning whether traditional marriage is the basic means for sustaining the social structure, or even a necessary institution for providing what many consider the inescapable emotional needs of the individual—love, affection, caring, sharing, intimacy.

Psychiatrist Roderic Gorney, in *The Human Agenda,* says that from babyhood on, we in the Western world have been overfed and overstimulated on a diet of intense emotional relationships so that what is actually an artificial need is experienced as a basic, urgent, almost physiological one. Intense emotional involvement—with mother, father, siblings, friends, and later lovers, spouses and children—is so taken for granted that questioning it would seem to be denying our need for such essentials as food, water, and oxygen.

Gorney compares this need to the way babies, from birth, are given ready-made baby food prepared with large quantities of salt and sugar. Obviously, as they grow up they demand sugar and salt in similar large quantities in their diet, insisting it is the "natural" way food should taste when in actuality it is an acquired taste.

Although cross-cultural studies rarely prove anything to everyone's satisfaction, one can see in them useful alternatives. Tahiti, before it was partially Westernized, and the Marquesas Islands in the South Pacific both have a different interpersonal tradition. In these societies the mother and father attempt in every way to "cool" the relationship between themselves, as parents, and the children by having the children's needs met by members of the extended tribal family. Various forms of communal child-rearing have also been practiced in Scandinavian countries, in Israel, and by experimental social groups in the United States.

Although results from studies are not yet conclusive, children growing up in such societies seem to require far less intensity, closeness, what we call "tenderness," and emotional involvement from other people in order to be happy. Thus they experience a personal relationship quite differently than we do—particularly with a lot less possessiveness and jealousy. Most of all, they seem to have no need for the romantic dream that some day one perfect person will come along who will magically change their lives. Perhaps in all that "cooling" they learn easily and instinctively what we Westerners have to reach for—the idea that the only person who can change your life is you.

In America we are only now beginning to perceive, for example, how our need for an intense, one-to-one emotional involvement is as socially conditioned as our taste for hamburgers and malts. It is thus no cultural accident that young people all over the country are actively experimenting with a variety of open marriages, group marriages, communes, multiple sex partners, and extended families. Compared with the total population, the number of experimenters is still very small, but numbers are not the essence of these movements.

It is not our intention here to debate the pros and cons of any of these issues. What needs to be emphasized is that the growing disaffection with marriage is largely the result of women's increased self-awareness, which in turn has altered the point of view of many men.

Also important is the recognition that many individuals in modern society experience the need to seek new means of finding fulfillment and that many of the old solutions—

specifically the traditional till-death-do-us-part marriage—no longer work for a large portion of the population. Interestingly enough, until someone dared question whether traditional marriage was actually meeting the needs of marrieds themselves, no one seriously advanced the idea that marriage might not be the ideal goal for everyone in society. Facing this possibility seems to be an effective first step to defusing the whole process.

GET THEE TO AN ALTAR

Everywhere one looks, it is a couple's world. It is as if there were a conspiracy—which we call "pairing pressure"—to keep it that way. Books, magazines, counselors, therapists sell one message to unmarrieds: "Shape up, go where other singles are, entertain more, raise your sex quotient, get involved, get closer, be more open, more honest, more intimate, above all find Mr. Right or Miss Wonderful and *get married.*" Even books supposedly extolling the single life are in reality thinly disguised how-to manuals concerned with making do until the right person is found. Seldom do singles find the suggestion that a single is anything but an incomplete couple or that singlehood can be a fulfilling, rewarding, freely chosen life-style, rather than a fearful, lonely waiting ground for marriage.

Even in sociology books and journals, where the writers should know better, singles as a group are ignored as a meaningful segment of society, even though in numbers they constitute more than one-third of the adult population. Inevitably they are thought of as either premarried people or the unfortunate residue of death or divorce.

Singles who are so distressed at not having found a mate

that they seek professional help discover that being single in itself is tagged immature by many experts, who then try to persuade the poor outcast that the solution to all his other problems lies in ceasing to resist the pairing pressure and in getting married.

One best-selling "authority," Dr. David Reuben, sells singles short by viewing singlehood as a fate-imposed interlude for biding one's time and boning up on strategy and mate-catching techniques. Sometimes this attitude is so subtly veiled it is barely discernible. Other times it is grossly, unbelievably blatant.

According to his book *Any Woman Can . . .*, Dr. Reuben apparently thinks every woman can find love and sexual fulfillment, but only if she is married. He puts down never-married women as "carefree little girls who don't want to be grown-up women" and suggests that they reject candidates for marriage "because they do not live up to their unrealistic expectations." A divorced woman, he says, "ought to be married." Then "she can have her chance for true happiness and make her second marriage everything her first marriage should have been."

Single men don't fare any better with Dr. Reuben. He characterizes them as "professional bachelors . . . always charming, always engaging. . . . Everything about them is exciting, flashy and marvelously in, but they are 'emotional freeloaders.' . . . The world's most accomplished time-waster is the perpetual bachelor."

For widows, too, Dr. Reuben has advice. He prods them back into marriage with these words: "A woman over the age of forty is almost certain to deteriorate emotionally (and sexually) if she is out of emotional (and sexual) circulation for too long. Even worse, the older she gets the faster the deterioration proceeds. Human beings are sexual beings and without the constant stimulation of regular and frequent sex they tend to fade and dry up."

Dr. Reuben represents some of the precise kinds of pressures that singles are up against. He is talking about stereotypes, not people. Obviously, while some unmarried women are immature, others are independent, self-sufficient, loving, interested in their careers, and not necessarily eager to give any of these up, which marriage might force them to do.

His statements are obviously not established facts. Regular sex indeed! Surely it cannot have escaped Dr. Reuben's attention that some of the people who have the most "regular and frequent sex" are also the most disturbed. Frequency of sexual intercourse, in and of itself, is no guarantee of mental health. If it were, the most successful gigolos and prostitutes could hang out a shingle announcing an additional specialty. It is not the frequency of sexual relations that determines one's health, but how one manages the totality of one's existence, with or without "regular and frequent sex."

And there are others like Dr. Reuben. In an otherwise good book, *The Ability to Love,* clinical psychologist Allan Fromme says: "It is also obvious that many young people who pride themselves on their selectivity are actually demonstrating that they would rather be alone. *Indeed, it is better to get married* [our italics]. Even if the marriage turns out to be a mistake, it is more of a mistake not to make this mistake. The longer an individual remains unmarried, the longer he is avoiding a commitment, detaching himself, unrelating himself to other people. And the more he is courting that permanent detachment that we call loneliness."

This statement certainly represents pressure-to-pair refined to its quintessence. Most of us have an idea how horrible a bad marriage can be, but if being alone and unmarried is *so* horrible, *so* devastating, *so* threatening that marriage—*any* marriage—is preferable, then there really isn't any choice at all—is there? At least, this has been the reasoning of generations of singles and the experts who have advised them. How many millions of people abandon real selectivity and choice in the face of this attitude we shall never know, but we hope that this book will expose the pressures, the falsehoods, and the myths that conspire against the single so that this panic-to-pair can be eliminated.

PRESSURE FROM YOUR PARENTS

One problem that is invariably brought up for discussion in "Challenge" workshops, especially by never-married men and women, is this: What do you do when you want to remain single but your parents continually pressure you to get married? Your reaction to that pressure—guilt over disappointing your parents, annoyance, anger, or resentment—can be a major barrier to living a free life.

If you are a victim of this pressure-to-pair, which often continues into the single's thirties, forties, and beyond, what can you do about it? The first step in coping with the problem is for you to understand how your parents feel and why they feel as strongly as they do. Various factors may influence their thinking.

First, they may believe in the myth that everyone ought to be married. Many parents are still burdened with the notion that if their children are not married, something must be wrong with them.

Furthermore, when they see the children of their sisters, brothers, and friends getting married while their own children are still spinsters and bachelors, this "success" of other parents makes them feel they themselves have somehow failed. They ask: "What's wrong with us that our children didn't get married too? Where have we failed as parents?"

Parents sometimes fear that if their children are not married, they may end up in a relationship not sanctioned by society ("swinging," living together, living in a commune). This in itself might be cause enough for concern if it were kept secret, but some parents also fear that other people will find out about it and condemn them as parents. They are concerned about their own image as well as their children's.

If their own marriage was a bad one, they may fear that this negative image of marriage provided a poor example and prevented their children from ever wanting it for themselves. If theirs was a good one, there is all the more reason why they might push marriage.

Parents may also wish their sons and daughters to marry because marriage signifies that their children are no longer their responsibility. They see their children's marriage as the conclusion of their job as parents and the beginning of a new freedom.

Another reason many parents urge their children to marry is that they look forward to the fun of having grandchildren. Grandchildren may also represent their own immortality, and they may feel sad about the prospect of the family name dying out.

Very often these fears, hopes, and feelings of failure are not consciously recognized by parents. Nevertheless, anxiety causes parents to pressure their children as they agonize over the question: "Is there something wrong with our children, or with us, that they don't want marriage and a family?"

As in resolving all conflicts, talking it out is vital in clearing the air. Even though your mother and father may be your friends, they are still your parents. Their friendship cannot be the kind of friendship that you have with your peers because, try as they may, there is no way for your parents to be totally objective about you. They are too emotionally involved—as parents—to be able to see things as you do on all occasions. Realizing this, sit down and explain to them as patiently and sympathetically as you can that you must lead your own life the way you think best, that marriage is not for you and—most importantly—that the fact that you are not married is not a failure on their part. This is exactly what Janice told her parents:

"Please try to understand. I know you would like me to be married, but I don't want it. Being single is a happy way of life for me. I'm not missing out on anything I want in my life. I have a good job. I have friends. I have goals I want to pursue. I can pick up the telephone and be with friends whenever I want to or I can be alone and enjoy that. I know you want me to be happy, and this is my way of being happy. You must try to believe this—because it's true. You have not failed me as parents. In fact, you have been wonderful parents because you have given me the freedom to search out and find the kind of life that is right for me—and that life is being single and happy. And if you think about all this for a little while, I think you will understand and be happy for me too."

In some ways your parents will tend to see you as a child, no matter what your age or how much they respect your ways. If they strongly want you to get married and you don't, they may experience this emotionally as disobedience, even though logically they may know better. For you to assert that you want to remain single in the face of such opposition is the ultimate declaration of your freedom and independence.

What is most important is how strongly you feel about

your decision. You are still the one who has to live your life and make your decisions. The more certain you are of what you want, the quicker others, including parents, will come around to your point of view.

THE ETERNAL SEARCH

Despite the incontestable satisfactions to be found in a partner of our choice, there is plenty of evidence to suggest that an all-out search for such a person simply doesn't work. In fact, the search for the one-and-only may well be the most handicapping of all of the mental "programs" with which a single saddles himself. Many singles decide what they will do for a living, where they will work, where they will travel, and what they will do for recreation, driven by this search alone.

George and Elaine told of their single-minded devotion to the search in a "Challenge" workshop.

At the beginning of his hospital internship in a new city, George, a young unmarried physician of twenty-nine, moved into a singles' apartment complex with the express purpose of meeting more women—specifically the one-and-only. He felt it would be good for his career to marry, he felt he was ready to marry, and since he had not met the right woman during his long training, the move seemed like a good idea.

He hadn't counted on the incessant activity, the endless parties and socializing, the omnivorous "relating," nor the women who were as intent on meeting and marrying him as he was on meeting and marrying one of them. After several months of participating in and witnessing the frantic pairing activity, he realized with a shock that what he really wanted was not necessarily to get married but to have what is frequently described as a "meaningful relationship." He wasn't sure what the right way to find that might be, but he was certain that it should not include filling his life exclusively with this endless marital hunting game.

He moved into a small house which had a workshop where he could start making his own wood furniture, something he had always enjoyed. Although busy at the hospital and able to go out very little, he began pursuing his own interests instead of the one-and-only. One evening, attending a lecture at a nearby observatory, he met several interesting people, one of them a woman with whom he became good friends.

Whether he marries or not, he says, is no longer something that is so much on his mind. "When and if it happens, it happens. My views have done a 180° change, and my life is full. My only reason for marrying would be if I met someone with whom I would want to build a life together. I know for sure that that person would have already built one for herself —separately."

For the past three years since her divorce, Elaine, a librarian of thirty-four, had been returning each summer to a singles' resort in the mountains. She didn't particularly like the resort, but she had heard it was a great place for meeting men and she was increasingly desperate and intent on finding someone who could take her out of her single existence. The only trouble was things never seemed to work out romantically for Elaine. They would sometimes begin well but always fizzled disappointingly at the end.

"Then two things happened to set me straight," she says. "A man I was dating at the resort, whom I really liked, turned to me one night and said the most surprising thing. He said, 'Elaine, I don't think you really know how strong you come on with people—especially men. You've got the whole thing plotted there in your eyes—the desperate need to be wanted, the relationship, the marriage—the whole script. And you seem to want it so bad you could cry. I'm only telling you this because you're a nice, interesting woman when you aren't caught up in that Big Romance game. You should cool it—you frighten men away.' I didn't know what to say, I was so flabbergasted, but when I thought about it later, I knew he was right.

"The other thing that happened was that I met a woman who had just returned from a trip alone to Japan. She was bubbling over with her adventures, and it suddenly dawned on me that this was precisely what I really wanted from my vacations—and my life. This kind of freedom and independence! I'm already planning my first trip alone. Meeting someone will be nice, of course, but it will be frosting on the cake, not the cake itself."

Both George and Elaine were trying in the beginning to build their lives around the time-honored single goal of finding a mate. As a result, their lives quickly became lopsided and unsatisfying. Since they were committing the cardinal mistake of the single state—failing to see themselves as complete people—they were paying the price and becoming incomplete people by not fulfilling their own potential.

THE MAGIC ONE-AND-ONLY

One of the most sacred concepts of our society is the idea that the essential ingredient of happiness (especially for a woman) is to be married to the "right" person. Little girls learn that only the kiss of a prince will wake them to a happy-ever-after life, and little boys believe that a kiss from the right girl can transform them from frog to prince.

Later, young girls read that a knight on a white horse will

save them from a dragon, and boys learn that saving the right young lady will get them the hand of—surprise, surprise—the king's beautiful daughter.

These stories teach us that if we can just find the right person—*the one*—and save him or her (i.e., marry that individual) all our problems forever after will be laid to rest. The process starts in the early teens. Some sixth, seventh, and eighth grade children are going steady, and many of their parents encourage it and think it's cute. Even at this tender age, they are pushed into the search for the one-and-only. Traditionally, marriage in the Western world has been monogamous and death did one part. Although marriages now end in divorce much of the time, people still enter into marriage with the idea that it is a permanent relationship. Is it any wonder, then, that the search for the one-and-only can become such an all-pervasive element in the lives of so many unmarried people?

This search for the one-and-only is based on two basic errors and is generally self-defeating.

Error #1: There Is Only One Such Person

Of course, there is such a thing as love, and love is grand and we're all for it, but there are many people in the world with whom one might be deeply in love, and over the course of a lifetime, a fortunate person may find a number of such relationships. There is certainly not a single, solitary one and one only, in the whole universe, who alone is destined for "me and only me."

Error #2: Finding the One-and-Only Will Solve All Your Problems

It doesn't matter whether you're married or single, only you have the full and final responsibility for your life. If you find a perfect or nearly perfect mate, it is probable that you will have love and steady companionship, but finding such a person does not guarantee you satisfaction, happiness, or self-esteem—only you can do that for yourself. And the better you do it while you are single, the more assurance you have that you will be ready, not for the one-and-only, but, more realistically, for a person who may fulfill many of your needs and desires, even though he or she probably can't fulfill them all. Even if anyone could do all that, you would still have a lot to do for yourself to balance the relationship.

In trying so hard to find the one-and-only, you defeat yourself. In any psychological or physical endeavor, we know that trying too hard usually generates so much tension that it makes reaching the goal even more difficult. If almost everything you do is motivated by the search for the one-and-only, you will inevitably miss out on most of the other values and benefits to be derived from your experience and from the people you have overlooked because they were not the sought-after one.

Being human, we yearn for the comfort of arms, the warmth of a "perfect understanding and love." The longing can sometimes seem so powerful, so intense, that you would swear you *need* someone desperately. But if you analyze your feelings, you will see that what you so desperately *want* you don't necessarily *need.* To search ardently and compulsively for such a relationship is sure to narrow both your vision and your personality, thus virtually guaranteeing that you won't find it.

It is only when you stop or relax the search that you can allow another person to truly enter your life. Happiness, joy, delight in another—these are things that cannot be compulsively sought after. They are by-products of who you are and how intelligently you have developed your mind, your heart, and your spirit.

George O'Neill, co-author of the best-selling *Open Marriage,* put it simply: "You can't buy love, you can't make love happen; it's there because it's there, and the more you force or try to hold a person, the more you push him or her away."

In one "Challenge of Being Single" workshop, a twice-divorced woman of forty recited the frustrations of the one-and-only search to a never-married girl of twenty-seven: "Go on and kid yourself if you must, but I've been through it all and I know," she said. "I used to think, years ago, that there must be only one man alive who could understand me 'perfectly.' Well, no one ever did. How could they? How can anyone be expected to completely understand someone else? It was doomed before it started. And what is more, whenever I found a person who seemed to fit the bill, I so burdened down the relationship with shoulds, oughts and imperatives of undying love and devotion, I scared the poor guy out of his wits. What is worse, my eyes were so blinded by my urgency, I couldn't even see these men as real people, so I made some bad choices.

"I've calmed down a lot and I've stopped searching. But now I do things for myself and go places for my own enjoyment. I'm not worried. I'm still enough of a romantic to think that I may yet find the almost perfect guy, and if he does come along, this time we'll have a fighting chance. But if he doesn't, I'll still have a good life."

Usually singles can see this point logically, even if it takes a lot of work for them to arrive at it emotionally. The point is that only by cultivating your own personality, interests, and pursuits can you come anywhere near achieving the kind of personal independence that makes the start of a good relationship possible—and helps keep it going once you've found it.

A POSITIVE VISION OF THE SINGLE LIFE

In the four-year history of the "Challenge of Being Single" workshops, there has been a distinct change in the things that participants report about the satisfactions of the single life. Increasingly, both men and women in the workshops are becoming more vociferous about the joys of being free and the secure feelings of confidence that come from being on their own and self-reliant. It is not that these people are becoming less realistic about the problems of being single— they are still aware of them—but we are beginning to see a much more balanced outlook that includes a healthy amount of appreciation and optimism about their status, and far less of the defeatism that originates in large part from the unfairly negative mythology with which society has always burdened the single. (We will be examining some of that mythology in the next chapter.)

At the same time, little by little, we are seeing reflections of this new self-awareness in the popular media. For example, a magazine called *Single*, with an initial press run of 750,000, emerged late in 1973, aimed directly at this special market of newly aware singles. Shortly afterward, *Newsweek* ran a cover story about singles which described the flourishing new singles-only institutions: the cruises, apartment complexes, weekends, celebrations, and clubs. It attempted to lay to rest the old "lonely-hearts" image of the single. Although the story was a prime example of a newsweekly-type announcement of an emergent life-style, as a whole it ended up doing little to dispel the lonely-and-waiting image of the single—a stereotype that should be laid to rest.

According to *Newsweek,* singles have discovered several dozen new ways to have fun, fun, fun, but behind all the "intensely ritualized" enjoyment, behind the drinking, dancing, sailing, and martinis, bikinis, poolside stereos, and saunas, there may be detected, if one just looks, the same old loneliness, despair, second-class personhood, and longing to be married. The implication is that it is probably okay to be fun-loving and single until you are thirty, but then, "Forget it! ... we know that you, behind that suntan, are single, lonely and you want to be married."

To the magazine's credit, it was aware of certain "new voices," the sociologists, psychologists, and others who have detected broad social trends in the single scene—people like Columbia University anthropologist Herbert Passin, who has said, "For the first time in human history the single condition is being recognized as an acceptable adult life-style for anyone. It is finally becoming possible to be both single *and* whole."

In our opinion, what is really happening is simply that some singles are beginning to discover the many advantages of single life on a deeper basis. They are making discoveries about self-identity and finally seeing singlehood as a unique opportunity to explore the possibilities of meaningful work, freedom, love, and caring relationships in a new way. Indeed, we may be on the verge of a generation which will put the search for self-identity above the quest for a mate.

This opportunity for personal growth is one of the biggest advantages of the single life, since singles are generally under less pressure to tailor-make their lives to the needs of others. Personal growth encompasses taking risks, being adaptable, learning about oneself and the world, accepting change—and ultimately even welcoming change as a source of adventure, fun, and fulfillment.

HONESTLY NOW, HOW COME <u>YOU'RE</u> NOT MARRIED?

In pursuit of self-identity, begin with the question that started this chapter: "How come *you're* not married?" Often a put-down when other people ask it of you, it can be of considerable value if you will ask it of yourself—and give yourself an honest answer. Usually the panic-to-pair precludes any analysis (calm or otherwise) of why, indeed, you are single, but the question is a legitimate one. By the same token, it should make just as much sense for you to ask the couples that you know, "How come you're married?" and have them respond seriously and with candor, so that you might both profit from the answer.

To explore the idea of "How come you're not married?" try answering a few questions. Do you think there's something wrong with you? Did you never meet "the right person"? Was "the right person" always unavailable? Did you find "the right person" and lose him or her? Could it be that you don't want the responsibility of children and are concerned that a mate will? Are you having too much fun? Do you love your freedom and privacy? Do you have a demanding creative and professional goal which requires time and concentration? Do you really want to be married or do you just want something that you feel only marriage can bring?

You may come up with both negative and positive answers, but after your own analysis, look at the following list of the most commonly mentioned pros and cons of being single that are brought up in "Challenge" workshops.

BALANCING ADVANTAGES AND DISADVANTAGES
OF BEING SINGLE

Following is a list of the most commonly mentioned advantages of being single that singles have talked about in "Challenge" workshops. Surprisingly, until singles begin to talk about it, most of them are not aware that there are so many advantages. Maybe there are some here you never thought of, and maybe even a few occur to you that you would like to add. Some may seem trivial to you, but to the people who mentioned them, they represented important aspects of the quality of their lives.

- ☐ Not having to explain where I've been
- ☐ Can stick to my own bad habits without having to put up with someone else's
- ☐ More privacy
- ☐ Freedom to pursue my own interests
- ☐ More chance to communicate with myself
- ☐ Can have friendships with many members of the opposite sex without the jealousy of a mate
- ☐ Can set my own schedule and activities without wondering what someone else will think
- ☐ Can make my own decisions without having to give in to or compromise with someone else
- ☐ Opportunity for a more varied sex life
- ☐ Can keep my home just as I like it (Don't have to clean house if I don't want to—as long as *I* can stand the mess!)
- ☐ More opportunity to try new things, new places, new ways of life

- ☐ Can end a relationship without the difficulty and expense of legally binding entanglements
- ☐ Can choose my own friends without wondering if a partner would like them or not
- ☐ No one to hassle me when I'm tired and out of sorts
- ☐ Not having to fix someone else's breakfast
- ☐ Can see the movies, plays, and TV shows that suit me—and not feel guilty
- ☐ More peace and quiet—no bickering and fewer tensions
- ☐ Can eat what I like, when I like
- ☐ An opportunity for a wider variety of experiences than possible in marriage
- ☐ No pressure to have children
- ☐ Can spend as much time as I want doing what I like—including my work
- ☐ Having no in-laws to fight with

As you know all too well, there are also disadvantages. Before we're done, we plan to show you how to turn as many negatives as possible into positive aspects of your life.

- ☐ Having no significant person who really cares what I do, what I feel, what I think about
- ☐ Loneliness—not being able to depend on companionship
- ☐ Being odd person out at dinner parties and most other social events
- ☐ The lack of sharing—of owning things in common, whether a house or a record album, or sharing memories, places, events
- ☐ Being pitied by well-meaning friends

□ Higher cost of being single (higher taxes, cooking for one, etc.)

□ Lack of a regular sex life—sometimes feast, sometimes famine

□ Feeling left out because it's a couples' society

□ Having no one to brag to about my successes

□ Heavier responsibilities in taking care of everything by myself—living quarters, car, clothes, marketing, etc.

□ Less certainty about my future

□ Having to suffer discriminations against singles

□ The implied suggestion there's something wrong with me, and general embarrassment over my single status

□ Getting through holidays and weekends

□ Being alone when I'm sick

□ Missing the emotional closeness of someone of the opposite sex

□ Having no one to come home to

□ Having no one to make plans with

□ Being forced to think in terms of a "sex life" so far as the opposite sex is concerned, instead of a fully rounded friendship, such as marriage should be

□ Eating alone

Of course, your list will vary somewhat, depending on your age, economic status, whether you are never-married, divorced, separated, or widowed, and whether you have children.

When singles are together talking about their lives, one of the things that always stands out is the relativity of advantages or disadvantages. What one single may regard as "just awful" or a "disaster" is something another single takes in his stride, doesn't mind at all, or actually views with delight and anticipation.

One thirty-year-old divorced mother told us that she "wouldn't dream of going to a movie alone" (presumably because of feeling lonely or seeming to be the object of pity), but she never minds staying home or returning to an empty house.

Another divorced woman, about fifty, who had left her husband after thirty years of marriage, said that she could go anywhere alone, didn't mind it, in fact had done a lot of it while she was married, but she hated, above all else, opening the door and walking into an empty apartment.

One widower finds great joy in cooking for himself and his friends, while a divorced man of forty-five, a scriptwriter, is so uncomfortable in the kitchen that he eats out every night or goes without meals at home rather than cook for himself. One single's bane is another's boon.

Different relationships and situations exist in individual single lives or specific marriages, but in a broad way here's what we see as the overall general advantages of being single contrasted with those of being married:

SINGLE	MARRIED
Privacy	**Companionship**
Being able to think and create without interruption in a peaceful atmosphere	Being held and loved; feeling another's presence; hearing another's voice
Time	**Family**
Having time to travel, cultivate talents, relax, entertain, be entertained	Having children and sharing in their care; having grand-children as you grow older

Freedom

Being able to choose, to make decisions, to form friendships, to use your time as you wish

Help

Sharing the work; having another point of view when making decisions

Opportunity

Being able to extend borders of friendship, develop skills, move to new jobs and new places

Care and Security

Having someone to look after you; having greater financial support

Weigh and balance these pros and cons of singlehood and marriage for yourself and see what you come up with. You will probably stumble on ideas and insights that will surprise you. To sum up: The single life can be—and for many single people, is—a realistic alternative to marriage, with many positive aspects unavailable to married people.

Never forget that an altar is also a place where sacrifices are performed. There's no reason why you, as a single, can't take the flame—and leave the ashes.

2. Myths and Discriminations

In discussions with thousands of individuals in "Challenge of Being Single" courses over the past few years, it has become apparent that society's attitudes toward singles cluster around several specific notions or ideas—myths, if you will—about the nature of single people and the character of their lives. These traditional beliefs tend to perpetuate an essentially negative and unfair image of the single life. As with all myths, there is an element of truth concealed in them somewhere, but they do a great deal of harm when all singles are assumed to fit these stereotypes and when singles themselves shape their own self-images from them. Let us briefly examine what these myths are so that we can first recognize, and then deal with them.

Myth #1: All Single Women Want to Get Married

More never-married women than divorced or widowed women say they want to be married, and, indeed, over 94 percent of the never-married women do marry by the age of forty-five. This is testimony to society's all-powerful pressure-to-pair, and, to be fair, to the appeal of the married state as well.

But what these figures fail to indicate is that a large number of this same group will also end up being divorced or widowed—some two, three, or even four times. In addition, the divorce rate continues to increase so that, at the present time, one in three marriages ends in divorce, and but for a variety of practical and cultural pressures, obviously many more would end that way. A corollary to this myth would seem to be: half of the married women wish they weren't.

Since women continue to have fewer options and less freedom than men, the vast majority of women will continue to opt for marriage, at least for a while. But there are signs everywhere that change is in the air. Both men and women are marrying somewhat later in life, and while marriage still remains an attractive goal, *especially to the unmarried,* more and more young women are aware that there are alternatives and are responding wholeheartedly to new life-styles and opportunities.

Currently about half of all single women have been married before, and it is significant that once a woman is divorced or widowed she is in no big rush to remarry. Many flatly state that they do not want to remarry at all. In "Challenge" workshops they remark, "Once is enough for me." This antimarriage bias is suggested by 1970 U.S. Census statistics which show that more than one-third more divorced women than men had *not* remarried at the time the census was taken.

Surprisingly, this was true for women under 45 years of age as well as for older age groups, where one might expect more women to remain single simply because, statistically, they have less opportunity to remarry because there are fewer men in this age group left in the population.

Many once-married women say quite firmly that they don't want to remarry at all. Their reasons reflect not only the desire to avoid the problems that bring about divorces in the first place, but also their intention to take advantage of the greater freedom being afforded women in today's society.

Barbara, a widow for two years, sums it up this way:

"I worked when I was married, just as I do now, but then I also had to do all the cooking, take care of the house and do all the endless chores for two people instead of one. Don't get me wrong. I loved Fred, but now I have so much more time to do things. I used to feel tired all the time trying to do two jobs—working outside and inside the house, too. Women's lib just hasn't filtered down enough to really change things, at least not yet. I've never met a man yet who is really willing to share the household chores. So I'm going to enjoy my freedom and stay single."

Additionally, the partial acceptance of a variety of non-marital, live-together relationships between people of all ages allows women who want intimate male companionship without marriage to have it, within the structures of society. Women today are more aware of the personal price they may have to pay in many marriages, and are a little less willing to pay it. Ultimately this awareness will not only change the nature of marriage, it will change the number of marriages as well.

Myth #2: All Confirmed Bachelors (Single Men) Are Afraid of Responsibility

This idea may seem dated to you, but there are still plenty of people around who hold to it. If all women are predators, hell-bent to trap a man, then naturally all uncaught men—the quarry—must be running for their lives. It is true, of course, that some single men are afraid of marriage—the intimacy, the commitment and the responsibility—but these are not problems for the majority of single men. They are, however, problems that frequently cause marital woes for men who commit themselves in spite of these feelings.

The problems (if we must call reasons for remaining single "problems") emerge in statements that range from "I want to keep my freedom in order to pursue personal interests" to the more banal one of "I've just never found a girl I want to spend the rest of my life with." Paul, a thirty-five-year-old inventor-businessman, didn't discover how important a period of freedom actually was to his work until life forced him to make a choice.

Paul says: "I learned something important about myself quite by accident. I had had a long-time relationship which was certainly equivalent to marriage. So I knew I wasn't afraid of the responsibility—on an emotional level or on the financial one. But when Jill finally made an issue of marriage, I realized that I just didn't want to get married—then—and we split up. All along I had thought that I wanted to get married—because it seemed the thing to do—but only when the chips were down did I see that I really wanted time for my work."

Another subtle, more hidden truth lies embedded in the second reason: "I've just never found a girl I want to spend my life with."

Vic, a never-married forty-five-year-old industrial designer, talks about it this way: "I've had a number of good relationships with women through the years—in fact, I have one now. But I've truly never found a woman with whom I wholeheartedly wanted to share my life. Some of my friends think I'm selfish and a perfectionist. But I never planned it this way. It just happened. Perhaps I'm just more romantic than they are. Anyway, a few years ago when I first realized this, I felt puzzled and wondered if there was something wrong with me. After thinking about it a lot, I decided there wasn't. I may still get married. Who knows? But if I don't, it won't devastate me."

Of course, you can look behind such statements and imagine any number of secret fears or immaturities, and in some cases you may be right, but the reasons for which people get married are frequently no less immature than those for not getting married. In fact, when we deal with Myth #5, we will see that the mental health of singles is at least as good as that of married people.

What looks like fear on the part of men today may be no more than a heightened awareness of the many ways they can be involved in a relationship which they may not want to end in marriage. As in Paul's case, it may be no more than protecting, if only for the time being, the freedom they have come to value.

A twenty-seven-year-old never-married physicist, Stan is perhaps more typical of the single man who has been so busy getting his career started that he has simply not had time to develop in-depth friendships with women. He told a group of singles in a "Challenge" workshop: "I'm really bugged by well-meaning friends who kid me about not being married and suggest that I am 'afraid' to be married. Afraid? That's nonsense. Actually I am more than ready to get married, but I've been too busy working to cultivate the kind of social life that leads to marriage. I had to work my way through college and put my younger sister through school on my salary. What with paying back all the accumulated debts and working overtime, I just haven't had a chance to meet many women—

let alone pursue a relationship to the point where I care deeply enough to marry."

Stan's comment, far from revealing any fear of marriage, reflects what we feel is a significant, growing trend for both men and women in our society. Getting married is becoming something one chooses to do or not to do, not something one *must* do in order to lead what society has deemed a complete life. Stan implied that when he is ready he may, or he may not, get married. It is an open proposition.

An increasing number of men (and women) are also opting for singlehood because they don't want to lose their identity. A thirty-two-year-old editor named John began by discussing the myth that single men fear marriage: "Yes, I think the myth still exists, but look at the places where it is still going around—TV situation comedies, commercials, B movies, and mass magazines. Anyone who's been paying attention to the changes in real people, at least those of my age, during the last few years can't possibly believe what they read and see.

"Four years of marriage taught me that living with a woman is nice, but that marriage itself is not an institution that makes any sense to me personally. It's not that I'm afraid of the commitment. I love the thought of being committed to another person. It's just that putting it down in writing and having it legally approved with a marriage certificate is irrelevant, and maybe bad for the relationship in the long run.

"Sure, it's my own personal view. But I have five close male friends, and only one is married. I think the single ones would all say something similar. Also, I think we have all been enlightened by some of the 'liberated' women on the subject of marriage. We agree that it's ridiculous that women should have to give away their identity when they get married, but men are beginning to realize that they lose some of their identity, too. Suddenly you become a husband locked into a supposedly permanent marriage. Who needs it?"

John's view is certainly not universal among single men in his age group, and many who have said similar things in the past have ended up getting married at the first opportunity; however, it appears that the myth in question is at least in need of revision.

Myth #3: It Is Easier for Men to Meet Women Socially Than It Is for Women to Meet Men

This myth is widely believed, but whenever singles discuss the subject, it always comes as a big surprise to the women to learn that the men feel they have just as much trouble meeting desirable women as women do meeting men.

Gregg, personable, intelligent, and almost thirty, was unequivocal in maintaining that he and his friends have a lot of trouble meeting interesting women: "I'm an engineer and the nature of my work means I only meet other engineers. There are very few women in engineering, and almost all of these are already married. I work long hours and just don't have a chance to meet many single women. I've tried the bar scene, but it's not for me. After the few blind dates set up by my friends, I've decided I never want to go out on any more of those. But I'd really like to meet someone interesting if I knew how. Some of my married friends just refuse to believe it is so hard to meet desirable women when you are single."

Gregg is not an exception. In fact, the problem seems equally true for men of all ages, backgrounds and professions —from MDs to bricklayers. Of course, we acknowledge that men have tradition on their side in being the social aggressor and instigating the casual encounter. Aside from meeting women at parties or having friends match-make for him, it is still more acceptable for a man even in these partially liberated times, to strike up a conversation with a woman than for a woman to strike up a conversation with a man. In that sense, it is easier for men, but (and this is an important *but*) the truth is that many men do not exercise their advantage of being the social aggressor in these obvious situations because of embarrassment or because they fear that they will be rejected as wanting nothing more than a pick-up and a quick and temporary sexual encounter.

In point of fact, a woman who really wants to be picked up has dozens of ways to let a man know she is available, and if she doesn't want to see him again, she has as many ways to get rid of him. A man, however, whatever his intentions, must take the first step, which is not always easy, and he puts himself in the position of a possible ego-deflating turn-down. In pick-ups it's a buyer's market.

Indeed, the very idea that all men want to do is pick up women is really a put-down for men because it perpetuates the notion (once deeply drummed into all growing girls) that men are just "out to get you" and that "all men want is sex." This concept has probably done more to foster tension and game-playing between male and female than any other myth. The unhappy consequence has been not only to perpetuate misunderstandings between the sexes but also to make many men feel that they *must* approach every woman as a sexual adversary to be conquered.

Myth #4: All Unmarrieds Are Terribly Lonely

This idea, in fact, is so widespread one can scarcely pick up a book or article about singles without being assured of its truth. Without minimizing the intense distress that loneliness can create for some people, experience with singles has shown that a large number are simply not as forlorn as this myth makes them out to be. Many are no lonelier than unhappily married people whose normal, human sense of isolation and loneliness can be accentuated by having an unloved and unwanted companion always present. According to the findings of the 1970 Census, just over 12 million of the 43 million singles actually lived alone. We see this in the workshops too: a large percentage have children or room-mates (of the same or opposite sex) or live with relatives. Because the subject of loneliness is so important to most single people, we explore it in depth in Chapter 4.

Myth #5: Single Life Is Hazardous Because There Will Be No One Around to Help You If You Are Hurt or Sick
It is one of the realities of life that married people do have help close by when they are troubled or ailing, and there is no denying the fact that this can be an enormous source of comfort. So when couples discuss singles, one of the first things they feel sorry about is the lack, in single life, of the constant physical presence of someone who cares. They can-not honestly imagine how one can get along without the immediate care and concern of another person.

Those singles who manage most successfully seem to have cultivated a few close friends they can count on when they are hurt or sick. Friends are important to everyone for a great many reasons, but probably even more important to singles because of this greater need in time of trouble.

But important as friends are, we should not lose sight of the undeniable fact that singles *are* on their own. Living completely alone may occasionally prove hazardous, but for some, the knowledge that no one is immediately available motivates them to take better care of themselves. Once you start depending on your personal resources for your own security, you will discover an enormous source of satisfaction and comfort. Self-reliance is undoubtedly one of the most important attributes for a successful single life.

Are singles less healthy than marrieds? In point of fact, actuarial tables show that they don't live as long as marrieds do. But when you start analyzing the available data, some curious facts emerge. A 1970 U.S. Department of Public Health study, *Selected Symptoms of Psychological Distress,* which was three years in the making, reports that never-married people suffer less than marrieds from headaches, dizziness, heart palpitations, insomnia, nightmares, nervousness, psychological inertia, feelings of impending nervous breakdown, and actual reported breakdowns. The widowed and divorced, however, suffer these symptoms about as frequently as marrieds. Never-marrieds, particularly females, come off extremely well in this study. In fact, the results were so favorable to the never-married (and so contrary to popular mythology) that they made headlines everywhere in the country.

Just *why* married people tend to live longer than the divorced, widowed, or never-married is open to debate. Alex Comfort, the British gerontologist and sexologist, believes "The reason is almost certainly lack of nurturance [among singles] —the psychological and physical support that married people give each other."

This may be the case, or it may be something as simple as the fact that married folk remind each other to make and keep doctor's appointments.

But what about the nurturance singles get from their friends? Perhaps this nurturance is of even greater worth, considering the many nervous disorders that plague marrieds. The complete answer probably lies hidden in a morass of relevant statistics, such as age, income, occupation, urban or rural residence, and race.

To put it somewhat bluntly, the accumulated evidence seems to be saying, "If you want to be more tranquil, your best bet is to stay single. If longevity is your goal, and you don't care that you may be in for greater stress, get married."

But statistical facts are not individual truths. No statistic need be true for you as a single unless you make it true for you. And the same applies to marrieds. A marriage license will not automatically guarantee you four or five extra years of life, just as you needn't make plans for an early wake just because you are single. As with everything else, you alone can determine the kind of health statistic you are, depending upon the tender loving care you give yourself.

What do these myths add up to? A total picture of singles as immature, selfish, and irresponsible. And more than just adding up to bad press for singles, these oft-repeated misconceptions contribute to a final, crushing indictment leveled by society at singles—namely, that they are, in some way, "sick." Why? The logic is impeccable: if they weren't immature, selfish, and irresponsible, they would be married, that's why.

THE END RESULT: DISCRIMINATION

If the myths we have been discussing remained only prejudices or abstract ideas without relationship to the real world, it would be unfortunate but of small cause for concern. However, these erroneous beliefs have led to very real discriminations which married people may be unaware of, but which singles feel sharply in a number of areas: taxes, jobs, loans and credit, housing, even insurance. There are few statistics on these discriminations because they are almost always covert leftovers from the days when singles were considered even more undesirable, and society did even more than it does now to encourage marriage. In some cases, legislation is being considered to get rid of them, and singles would do well to support various groups working toward this.

Taxes—Why Two Can Live as Cheaply as One

When the first federal income tax laws were passed in 1913, only couples from those states where, by law, each spouse owned one-half of the couple's property and income were able to divide their tax bill and pay at a lower overall rate. People in non-community-property states complained about this, and the outcry finally got Congress to change the law (in 1948) so that couples everywhere could split the family income and obtain the tax advantage. This eliminated advantage based on *where* people lived and switched it to *how* people lived. Perhaps the thinking was that the single person would be spending less money and therefore would have more left over, which the government would like very much, thank you. Aside from being patently unfair, this reasoning has worked real economic hardships as well, since many single people support aged parents or other family members and have other economic commitments that match those of a married person. But whether they have those commitments or not, their decision to remain single should not be the basis on which their taxes are calculated.

Until Vivien Kellems, the unmarried (by choice) fighting Connecticut Yankee, started her campaign in 1948, singles were paying as much as 41 percent more federal income tax than marrieds, on identical income. It was her relentless, one-woman battle against the Internal Revenue Service that finally caused Congress to pass the Tax Reform Act—but not until 1969. The tax was reduced, but singles are still taxed at a rate as much as 20 percent higher.

Janice, a forty-eight-year-old widow, was shocked when she had to pay her first income tax after her husband died. Her income was $8,000, on which she paid $1,590, but her married friend next door only had to pay $1,380 on the same $8,000. "I'm faced with the very same bills as when my husband was living: gas, electricity, maintenance, telephone, and everything else. So what I'm doing is handing Uncle Sam a $210 present just because I'm no longer married. It galls me!"

Harold, a bachelor, had a similar complaint. On his $16,000 income his tax was $3,830, while his married co-worker with the same income paid only $3,260. Along with the federal government, many states penalize the single with a higher tax rate. For example, in California a married person earning $14,000 in 1972 paid only $360 in state taxes, while a single person making the same amount paid $680.

How much can this cost you? In her suit against the government for this discrimination, Miss Kellems calculated that over a twenty-year period, Uncle Sam had collected almost $50,000 in extra taxes because she wasn't married. With interest, she figures the government owes her $100,000.

Is there anything you can do about this? Short of getting married, there are two possibilities. You can copy Vivien Kellems' idea—an updated version of our first tax rebellion in 1773 when angry taxpayers dumped tea into the Boston harbor—and send a letter accompanied by an old teabag to your congressman protesting the higher taxes. Surprisingly, a few years ago this stunt attracted a lot of press and brought the issue to the attention of some government officials.

Another effective procedure is to support COST (Committee of Single Taxpayers), a lobbying group in Washington, D.C., at 1628 Twenty-First Street, set up to fight this tax battle for singles. There is considerable public interest in the equalization of tax rates, and several measures are before Congress. If pressures are maintained, the chance is good that we will have fairer tax laws for singles before too long.

Jobs—The Executive Washout

In "Challenge" workshops when singles talk about getting jobs, many get quite indignant about discriminations that exist against singles in hiring practices. Most companies follow the general rule that married people are a better investment in terms of responsibility, dependability, and staying power. Often they are not the least bit hesitant in openly saying to employment agencies that they want marrieds only, since there is no law prohibiting discrimination based on marital status. Sex, yes. Race, yes. Marital status, no. There are exceptions, of course. Sometimes single men are actually preferred in fields like sales or insurance, which may require travel or night work. Single women are sometimes given preference over married women on the mistaken theory that they are necessarily more in need of work. Once hired, however, they often find that they are not taken seriously, the assumption being that they are only working until the right man comes along. Age, of course, plays a role in this.

Generally speaking, though, single men are often the last to be hired, the last to be promoted, and the first to be fired. This is particularly true in the corporate suite. The *Wall Street Journal* reports, for example, that only 2 percent of all top executives are single, while 33 percent of all adult males are single.

Frank, a personable forty-one-year-old engineer who had never married, complained: "Two months ago when our company lost a big contract we were counting on, they had to lay off several men and I was one of them. What makes me mad is that I had been with the company for almost five years and the man they kept on in my equivalent position had been there only three, but he was married. Our educational background and experience were almost the same, but in the end, I was the one who was booted out. They wouldn't admit it openly, but I heard later that his being married made the difference.

"What makes it even more ironic is that they don't have any kids and his wife is an executive secretary, while I'm putting my younger brother through college."

Personnel officers, employment counselors, and placement agencies agree to the sad fact that married people are almost always preferred over singles.

What can be done about these inequities? If you are looking for a job, your best bet for advancement will be with the smaller companies. Usually, the larger and more established the company, the more entrenched is the pattern of preferential hiring and advancement for married employees. Also, various surveys indicate that firms in the East and South seem to be the most antisingle. The Midwest is somewhat better, and the West is best of all, probably because it is generally less tradition-bound.

Seek a job with newer and smaller companies which are eager for growth and whose hiring practices are more apt to be based on talent, training, and experience rather than on marital status. And the happiest singles seem to be those who have found work in fields or professions in which they are self-employed.

Credit—No Loan If You're Alone

Martha, a widow in her early forties, and the head of her family with two children, wanted to buy a house. She discovered that in order to get a mortgage, it was necessary to have her father, seventy years old and living on a pension, co-sign it. Her signature was not enough.

However, Martha was better off than a thirty-year-old office worker who was flatly refused a loan because she was divorced. She was bitterly aware that even though her salary was more than that of a married male cousin, he had no trouble getting a loan for a similar size house in the same neighborhood.

And there's a sixty-year-old widow whose husband died four years ago. The companies with whom she had credit cards refused to let her change them over to her own name. Her solution? She continued to use the cards issued in his name because, as she put it, "Even a dead man has a higher credit rating that a woman."

Officials of various lending institutions, when questioned about their practices, usually say that everyone who applies for credit is treated equally. When confronted with the specifics of an individual case, however, they admit reluctantly that singles, especially divorced and widowed women, are regarded as being less financially responsible than married people.

Unfortunately there is a kernel of truth here, but it reflects less on single women's overall responsibility than on their ability to find good paying jobs that can support them. Said one forty-year-old divorcee, Carolyn, with two children "The psychological problems of being a woman alone are really child's play compared with the economic ones. I can cope with too much housework, too little time for myself,

dates that don't live up to expectations, but tell me, please—
how do I stretch a $135-a-week paycheck to cover rent,
dental bills, new children's shoes, and food prices that jump
higher every time I shop?"

Although Carolyn would probably not be a good credit
risk by anyone's standards, even single women who make as
much as $10,000 or more a year are often refused credit.

And it is not only the single female who is looked at with a
jaundiced eye when applying for credit. A never-married,
thirty-six-year-old male accountant with a good salary, who
had always lived in apartments but liked puttering around
with tools as a hobby, wanted to buy a house so he could
have a workshop. "The first thing the bank asked me was
'Are you married?' When they found out I was in the over-
thirty group and still not married, they acted as if I had
committed a crime. In the end they refused the loan, even
though my salary was higher than that of a married friend
who had gotten a similar loan a month earlier."

Married people are automatically assumed to be better
credit risks by banks, department stores, and mortgage and
credit card companies. It sometimes comes as a shock to the
newly divorced and widowed that once they are single, even
if they always paid their bills promptly and in full when they
were married, they become credit risks.

What can you do about all this? If you have been refused a
loan by one company or firm, don't give up. Although such
policies are usually determined high up in the corporate
structure, individual managers generally have some leeway in
making decisions. You may even find a divorced, widowed,
or never-married loan officer who will be understanding of
another single.

There is something else you can do. If it is possible for you to keep the same address and the same job for at least a year, preferably two, it will help you build a good credit rating. Loan officers frown on job hopping or moving to new living quarters every few months. Even though you are prompt at paying your bills, if you change jobs and apartments frequently, banks and stores tend to become suspicious and fear you may skip town, leaving them with bad debts.

One "Challenge" workshop participant said that over the years he had made it a point to bank with the same institution that handled his employer's account, even though it wasn't totally convenient. On a few occasions he had been able to use his employer's relationship with the bank to help him obtain a loan.

A single woman who had been refused credit took the most direct path. She caught a loan official off-guard by asking point blank, "Is this because I am single?" He was so surprised he answered, "Yes." She explained, with dignity, that although some singles might be poor credit risks, she wasn't, and asked if he would please reconsider. He did and she got the loan.

Don't minimize the value of writing your congressman. A Fair Credit Billing Act which prohibits discrimination against singles is pending in Congress and your representatives do listen when enough pressure is applied. You might remind them that singles are approaching one-third of the adult population and that their votes represent a large part of the electorate.

Housing—No Dogs or Singles Wanted

While housing is hardly as great a problem for singles as taxes, jobs, and credit, it can nevertheless be infuriating, painful, and humiliating.

The difficulty is that many landlords still assume that singles thrive on wild parties, are highly unreliable, and stay up all night disturbing other tenants. The truth is that singles, like most other people who work, are much too tired at the end of the day to indulge in endless partying.

At a workshop one day, Carol, an attractive, newly divorced secretary who had just been apartment hunting in a desirable west-side residential area of Los Angeles, blurted out with obvious anger:

"Would you believe that three different apartment managers refused to even let me look at their apartments when they found out I was divorced! They said they preferred married tenants, and they almost slammed the door in my face. You'd think I was a leper, the way I was treated."

In the face of such discrimination, what can you do if you are looking for an apartment? To start with, be as presentable and well groomed as possible. If you feel the rental agent is really worried about the level of reliability in singles, you might bring it out into the open and discuss it with him. If you can get good references from former landlords, do it. Then mention that you have such references to any prospective landlord.

If all fails, and if your preferences lean in that direction, you may want to look into the specific apartment complexes for singles. In these, of course, singles are welcomed with open arms. There are advantages—recreational facilities, more structured social events, and availability of other singles—which may appeal to you.

Insurance—Singles Are Against Our Policy

Insurance discrimination against singles follows much the same pattern as credit discrimination. Of course, this is not evident in life, health, or accident insurance, which is based more on age, sex, and occupational status than on marital status. But in auto insurance, single men under thirty usually must pay a higher premium than married men of a comparable age. However, this varies from company to company (a hopeful sign), and generally, single professional men pay lower rates. Single women, too, meet with the same discrimination, but in their case, twenty-five becomes the magical age when they suddenly become more "stable" and eligible for lower premiums in that silly world of insurance stereotypes.

The divorced come in for some special discrimination all their own. While the never-married can usually get insurance, even though it may mean paying a higher premium for it, the man or woman who has just been divorced may be refused insurance outright. Then, in most companies' views, one year after a divorce one automatically becomes a better risk. We asked several insurance executives how they could justify such a biased procedure, and they explained that divorced people are "emotionally unstable," that they "drink more heavily," and that "their accident rate is higher." One official, who had once been divorced himself, added, as if in justification, "And it's true . . . it's a difficult time right after a divorce . . . they do have more accidents."

Not *all* recently divorced people have more accidents, and therefore the blanket classification is patently false and unfair. If such a policy is to make any sense at all, it should be applied on an individual basis. That is, only after a person is known to be unstable or undependable should he be denied insurance or made to pay a penalty. This is the way it works with married people. Why should it be any different for singles?

Similarly, couples who live together without getting married are frequently turned down or forced to pay more for their policy from high-risk auto insurance companies. Once again, the official view is that unmarried couples are automatically "less stable," "more irresponsible," more likely to "split up and disappear at any time." Interestingly enough, most insurance companies exempt the widowed from such discriminations, treating them the same as marrieds.

In homeowners-tenants insurance, singles are usually allowed only a $250 deductible (on theft, fire, etc.) rather than the $100 allowed married people. However, when both members of a married couple work, some companies will only allow them the $250 deductible, presumably because, like the single, they will be home less often to watch their property.

What can you do about getting insurance at the lowest rates if you are single, especially recently divorced? Not a lot. Most of these rates and policies are fixed, and your agent does not have the power to alter them. What you should do is shop around. Some insurance companies are less discriminatory than others. One woman, a schoolteacher of thirty-two who had just become legally divorced (although she had been separated for two years), pointed out this fact to an insurance executive and showed him letters of reference from her banker and school superintendent. She was so persuasive that she got her insurance at an appropriately lower rate. With shopping and persuasion, you may be able to save yourself a few dollars.

IT'S OKAY TO BE SINGLE

Throughout much of this chapter we have been viewing the major discriminations, but singles are subject to a parade of small needling ones as well. For example: food packaged in family-size quantities is disproportionately more economical, and so singles end up paying more for food than marrieds; hotel rates for a single are generally almost as much as for a double; vacation package tours require singles to pay a supplement for a single room, unless they want to take a chance on pairing up with a total stranger. Perhaps most annoying are the inevitable pauses and puzzled glances from many people you meet when they learn you are single.

As a single, what do you do about the annoyances, binds, cubbyholes, categories, and cul-de-sacs into which a coupled world has placed you? We have already suggested a number of specific procedures, but these discriminations and myths which do, indeed, exist in the outside world can only really harm you when they exist in your own head as well.

By now it must be clear that everything conspires to make a single think, "It's wrong to be single." If you value yourself enough, you will make every effort to assert—to yourself and to the world around you—"It's okay to be single." With that understood, you can begin to fortify yourself with your own individualism and an appreciation of your own talents. The next chapter will help you do this. But for a quick summary of what this has meant to many singles, glance ahead to the Singles Manifesto at the end of the last chapter.

3. The Singles Community — One Third of the Nation

We have just taken a look at some of the myths about singles. Now, what are some of the truths? Singles pursue these truths in "Challenge" workshops, in search of what can be called the *single experience*—that is, of what it means to be single in a paired world, a citizen of the singles community.

Singles often come to the workshops believing that they have little in common with other singles in the group (the never-married, the divorced, the separated, or the widowed), but they emerge with the satisfying awareness that all singles, whatever their backgrounds, share much in the way of experiences, pleasures, and problems.

Singles have an enormous curiosity about how other singles solve the problems of singlehood—and both age and single-status differences begin to melt as the individuals talk, analyze, listen, and search for answers together. They begin to appreciate that their common concerns about loneliness, going out alone, facing society's prejudices, and coping with single life in a paired world—as well as their interests in making the most of the many opportunities and advantages of being single—outweigh the differences among them.

The differences among singles are illuminating too—and we will discuss them at length as we look at the practical problems facing different segments of the singles population. While you might be tempted to skip those which do not seem to apply directly to you, we think it would be more profitable if you read them all rather than reading solely about the problems with which you are already familiar.

It is not the purpose of this book to give advice on how to deal with all the day-to-day problems facing each of the groupings individually. There already exists, and we refer to it in the bibliography, a fairly large body of such material for the divorced, separated, and widowed. We only intend to point out some of the major emotional conflicts which each of these groups faces so that others not in those groups will be better equipped to understand their emotional needs.

The experience of singles in the "Challenge" workshops has been that they have learned as much from singles who seemingly have totally different problems as they have from singles whose problems outwardly resemble their own. For example, a thirty-two-year-old divorced man will share many problems with a forty-two-year-old widow when both have to raise children alone. And a thirty-eight-year-old never-married will be startled to find that he has many of the same problems as a fifty-five-year-old man who has just lost his wife.

Each kind of single has special feelings, unique to his or her circumstances. These are determined by age, sex, financial condition and, of course, whether the person has always been single or has recently entered the single state. For example, the never-married frequently see themselves as different from the formerly married and often will not even date singles in categories different from their own. They fear that they will not be understood. The formerly married sometimes feel that they would be uncomfortable being with someone who had never been married, that having once been a part of a couple, they have a particular set of experiences that only other formerly marrieds would understand. Similarly, the widowed, separated from their spouses by death, sometimes believe their feelings cannot possibly be understood by the divorced, who deliberately severed their marital bonds. And the widowed usually feel they would have even less in common with never-married singles.

To a great extent, we dealt with the never-married situation in Chapter 1. Now, let us take up the problems of the divorced, separated, and widowed, and of the single parent. We will show how all singles can share some common "solutions" to their problems—namely, the ability to accept change and take risks.

THE DIVORCED: A SENSE OF FAILURE

Perhaps what is most difficult for the newly divorced is going through an emotional upheaval at the very time they are having to work out a new life-style and find solutions to immediate practical problems: figuring out new budgets and financial arrangements, beginning a new social and sexual life, moving to another house or apartment, possibly settling the children into a new school, and, in the case of many women, having to find a job—all this and more, right when they are apt to be most unsure of themselves emotionally.

The most common state of mind experienced by the 5 million people in the country who are divorced, especially in the first year or two following a divorce, is a sense of failure.

If getting married is considered the most important social act for an adult, getting divorced is bound to be an admission of tremendous failure. Even when they have bitter accusations against an ex-spouse, they still ask themselves such questions as: What did I do wrong? What could I have done to make the marriage work? What's wrong with me that caused my marriage to fail?

This sense of failure is often accompanied by feelings of guilt for things left undone and for words left unsaid that might have saved the marriage. Anger and hostility toward the ex-mate are often the result of these emotions, which may be made all the more confusing by a residue of tender feelings that come at most unexpected times and cause painful second thoughts about the divorce itself: Should I have been divorced at all? Should I attempt to get us back together again?

These questions are even more difficult to answer when there are children whose welfare must be taken into account and whose presence (or absence) is a constant reminder of failure. This mix of conflicting emotions often creates an all-pervasive sense of worthlessness which goes well beyond the initial sense of failure. A man can frequently take refuge in a job. For a woman whose home and marriage were her whole life, the effect on her personality can be devastating as she gives up the romantic fantasies of a lifetime.

The First Year Is the Hardest

The result of this low estimate of one's self-worth is to push many divorced men and women in one of two distinct directions. Some newly divorced men and women withdraw from life as much as possible. These are often people who tend not to confide much in others. They even tend to stay away from former friends because of feelings of shame and a belief that no one can really understand them. Most of all, they want no part of going out and meeting the opposite sex. They have had enough of that and often vow at this early stage, never, ever, to marry again.

The course taken by others is to "play the field"—dating two, three, or four different people on alternate nights and keeping up a hectic pace in order to assuage momentarily the hurt, anger, and feelings of failure that haunt them. They are searching for someone—anyone—who might briefly provide them with diversion or a sense of being okay and not really a failure, someone who appreciates them.

It is at this period in divorced people's lives that they are vulnerable to anything or anybody that boosts their self-esteem. During the first few months to a year after a divorce—a time when one's good common sense is usually not operating well—many "rebound" into a second marriage, frequently repeating the mistakes of the first because they have failed to give themselves time to understand and accept their own contribution to the failure.

Mack, a sensitive young executive, noted this vulnerability of the newly single: "When I am dating a woman who has just been divorced, I am usually particularly careful to keep things as pleasant and unintense as possible—and for as long as possible. Oh, this doesn't mean I'm not turned on—but I try to 'cool' things. I feel this is the least you can do as a man. Some guys, of course, have always seen divorcées as 'fair game' of sorts and try to make the most of their emotional vulnerability. I don't. I remember how vulnerable I was the first several months after my own divorce."

From Rich to Poor—A Common Plight
Almost without exception women who are divorced complain that the biggest practical problem that confronts them

is having to adapt, sometimes quite suddenly, to a drastically lowered economic life-style.

Liz, a forty-year-old woman with a fifteen-year-old daughter, divorced from her lawyer husband after seventeen years of marriage, kept living in her Scarsdale estate. "But I couldn't pay even half the bills," she told us, "and there were times when I had to borrow money just to buy food to get through the week. No one could have guessed that I was counting pennies—I was still driving a Jaguar, wearing good clothes, and even going to a party or two, but I had very little cash. The new divorce laws really left me with almost nothing, especially since my husband is a lawyer—and no lawyer I talked to wanted to take him on for a courtroom battle. What is a woman like me to do? I've never been trained to make money. How do I begin again?"

There is, of course, no one answer. But we have included throughout this book a number of ideas and suggestions that singles themselves have found worked for them. In Liz's case, she began getting together with a singles group, where she learned that there is no substitute for direct action. She moved out of the estate into a small apartment, traded her Jaguar for a Volkswagen and began a course in real estate.

Liz, of course, represents the upper end of the economic scale, but among the middle class, divorce is frequently all that is needed to catapult a woman right out of a comfortable suburban house and into a one-room apartment—if not into the welfare lines.

In California alone, it is estimated that there are now half a million divorced, widowed, and never-married women who are heads of households, that is, women who have children and no husbands. Many of these are on welfare. In fact, Robert Moretti, Speaker of the California State Assembly, called this group "the most rapidly growing minority in the state." Usually, these women—often quite talented—can't find jobs that justify paying for a babysitter. Only vastly expanded opportunities for child care, education, and full- or part-time jobs for women can begin to make a dent in this problem.

It isn't only women who go from steak to spaghetti in the divorce courts. Men too, of course, suffer from drastically reduced and restricted budgets. And the fact that they find it easier to locate jobs and make money doesn't detract a whit from the pain and readjustment they must go through. Two can live as cheaply as one if they live together, maybe; if they live apart, never. If the divorced man begins a new relationship and must support a new family, the problem becomes even more excruciating.

Divorced men and women are often catapulted not only into a financial limbo, but into a social limbo as well. They face the problems of honing their social skills (which have undoubtedly fallen into disuse) and having to find and define a whole new identity as a single once they are no longer part of a couple. For example, they often have to cope with the embarrassment of going out alone to social gatherings and feeling awkward because everyone else is in couples. They are further embarrassed when starting to date again, not knowing how to act appropriately and feeling like an adolescent because they haven't been in such a situation for years. Such divorced people often feel alone, depressed, and "left out."

THE SEPARATED: A SENSE OF AMBIVALENCE

Being separated is perhaps an even more difficult state than being divorced. As a separated woman in a "Challenge" workshop described it, "I feel like I'm in prison. I'm not really married and I'm not really free. I'm suspended halfway between purgatory and hell."

The separated share many of the practical and emotional worries of the divorced, but their complicated social life adds an extra strain to all of these. In addition, it is often more difficult for the separated than the divorced to maintain their relationship with their mutual married-couple friends. Whose side is the couple on anyway—the husband's or the wife's? The couple itself doesn't always know and may be unable to take sides at all, which can make everything even more complicated.

An engineer in his thirties called being separated "a halfway point to the singles' world but with so many stresses and loose ends, it's hard to believe there's anything good over the horizon."

Among the 4 million separated people in the country, ambivalence is perhaps the most common feeling. Should we or should we not go back together? The nagging feeling persists that since the marriage is not yet terminated, there may still be a chance to save it. Ambivalence is one of the most trying and debilitating states in which one can exist. The indecision alone can trigger not only mental distress, but a number of physical symptoms—insomnia, weight loss or gain, severe fatigue, headaches, and gastrointestinal upsets.

Although, by being separated, one can continue to have some of the benefits of being married—for example, a better deal on income taxes, credit ratings, and job promotions—how it works out emotionally is often another matter. On the one hand, some separated, like the newly divorced, plunge into the excitement of new relationships and sexual experiences. They want to have their freedom and still be "safe." Since they're married, they don't have to get emotionally involved with anyone else. While this may be convenient in the short run, in the long run it may bring on a variety of unexpected problems.

Sarah, a forty-two-year-old writer, exemplifies another predicament a separated woman faces: "I thought we would just get separated and I would 'coast' for awhile—emotionally. After all, our children were grown. Harvey and I were still 'friends.' It wasn't so much that things were bad between us as they weren't really good. I had the idea that there should be more to life for me than that. And I wanted to try to find out what it was. The trouble was I never got the chance. I ended up having more marital troubles when I was separated than when I was married.

"First, Harvey ran into another car and we were both sued for $2,000. Then he moved in with someone briefly and brought his troubles with her to me. Up to a point, it was all very civilized. Then the matter of some jointly owned property came up. I wanted to sell and he didn't, so we fought over that. If we had been divorced, one or the other of us would have owned it. Then, he got sick and his girl friend was away, and so I had to see him through his hospital stay. He's okay now, but what worries me is—what if he had had a stroke or heart attack? I might have wound up with a wheelchair husband, back where I started from, and all because I didn't have enough courage to make a clean break when I had the chance."

Probably the greatest kindness the separated can do for themselves is to make the decision—either get back with their spouse and declare themselves married (even though the marriage may be far from what they'd like it to be) or make a break, go through the divorce, and declare themselves single. Only then, realistically, can they begin to launch a new life.

THE WIDOWED: A SENSE OF LOSS

For the widowed, who number just over 12 million in the United States—2 million men and 10 million women—the first year is the crucial time. During that period, the widowed typically experience a range of feelings, from an initial numbness and a sense of having died themselves, to anxiety, blame and anger, to a final acceptance of the need to get on with their own lives. This sequence seems to consist of three phases—impact, recoil, and recovery.

During that difficult first year, what it all adds up to is the need to do what might be called *grief work,* and the degree of success with which it is done by the widowed determines in large part their later readjustment. Essentially, doing the grief work means that the widowed face the task of talking out their mixed feelings, especially the intense distress connected with the grief experience. It also means working out the many new practical problems—money, work, housing, etc.—that confront them almost immediately.

While the widowed need friends with whom to talk out their bereavement, and while some friends do rally around, particularly during the first six months to a year, death is still very much a taboo topic in our society. Many people turn their backs on it rather than face the reminders of their own mortality. Consequently, some widowed find they do not get as much support as they would like—nor the kind of comfort they thought they would get—just when they need it most.

Nevertheless, grief and sadness are generally "acceptable" feelings, and the widowed are expected to express them. "Unacceptable" negative feelings, however, no matter how strongly they may be felt, are rarely permitted, and when expressed, are met with raised eyebrows and disbelief among friends and relatives. One such unacceptable emotion is anger toward the departed spouse, anger which also may broaden to include the world, society, or people in general.

"Why did you have to go and die and leave me all alone?" "Why didn't you care enough about me to take care of yourself so you wouldn't have gotten sick?" "Why didn't you explain your business to me so I wouldn't be so confused and feel so lost trying to understand it?" These are some of the angry questions widows may hate themselves for asking. But unless they recognize that they have this anger and somehow let it out, they will be unable to go on with their lives as fully as they should.

"I kidded myself when my husband died," said Mildred, a widow of fifty-four. "I was so overcome with what I thought was sorrow and remorse, I practically deified his memory for the first year or two. You would have thought he was an angel or a saint—everything he had said or done was 'perfect,' and he could do no wrong. Yet the truth is he was anything but perfect. He was careless, and we fought a great deal of the time.

"I bottled up this anger so much, it practically made me ill, and certainly a prisoner. What happened was this: I had a fire in the house. We had always had fire insurance, I thought. My husband had always taken care of it, I thought. It turned out he hadn't mailed the check for years, though he told me he had. It took my entire savings to repair the house. I was furious. But it broke the spell. After that I could see things in better perspective, and now I feel free to go on with my life."

Only a few widowed people will ever acknowledge that they feel a great sense of relief at the spouse's death when the marriage has been an unhappy one. Most people, of course, would not dare express relief, much less joy, at the passing of a spouse, but obviously in some cases this is the way a widowed person will feel.

Many widowed blame themselves in some fashion because the spouse died. "I should have spent more time at home with the wife and children, and maybe she wouldn't have had such a heavy load," a widower laments. "If I hadn't quarreled with him, maybe he wouldn't have driven so fast and had a head-on collision. I was the one who caused it!" said a widow. "If I had insisted he stop smoking, maybe he wouldn't have had a stroke!" . . . and the remorse runs on.

One way for the widowed to begin to overcome such guilt feelings is to realize that in marriage no adult human being can *make* another do something that he or she is not willing to do. You cannot make a person stop drinking or smoking if he really does not want to, and you cannot make him drive slowly. A person consciously or unconsciously makes his own decisions. If it seems you are making them for your spouse, it is only because he or she is acquiescing in one way or another with the decision making.

The Not-So-Merry Widow

We don't think it is an oversimplification to say that the most important goal for the widowed is to resume, as soon as possible, something that approaches a full, normal social life. However, people being what they are, there are often barriers in the way of that resumption. Sometimes, it is widowed's children who hold them back. In the case of Thomas, a widower of sixty, his married son and daughter did everything they could to keep him from dating, fearing that he would be "foolish," have his "head turned," get "taken"— and in the process, they would lose their inheritance. "It was only when I realized they were preventing me from living my own life that I put my foot down," Thomas recalls. "When I was firm enough, they stopped."

It is during the crucial first year after the spouse's death that the widowed are more prone to accident and illness than at any other time in their lives, and as we have said, for the first six months most friends and family usually do rally around the widowed man or woman giving aid, comfort, and support. Unfortunately, after this period, even friends of long standing begin to call less and less often, some even dropping the widowed person from their social calendar altogether. As with the divorced, there are many reasons for this. In "Challenge" workshops the "single-again" complain that the dropping is most often done by couples whose own marriages are shaky and who fear that the newly single person presents a threat. In addition, there is no denying that many marrieds feel more "complete" when they socialize with other marrieds.

"I couldn't believe it was happening to me," said Jane, a widow of forty-five. "I had known Ted and Helen for fifteen years and we had all been great friends when my husband was alive. During the first six months that I was a widow, Helen had been so concerned and caring. She had called often, invited me to their dinners, and even parties, though I didn't always go. When I did, I always brought a gift, or stayed later helping to straighten the kitchen or doing other things like that. Why was I doing it, I wondered? Was I trying to prove I had a 'right' to be there? Was I feeling unworthy?

"Anyway, I noticed there was tension growing, and one night I was drying dishes for Helen after a party, when she suddenly turned to me and said, 'Jane, I bet you have no idea how flirtatious you've become.' I was dumbfounded. She told me she noticed how I was 'playing up' to one of the men, but I sensed she was really talking about her husband. She was really telling me that she was afraid I would 'play up' to him. I protested, of course, because I had been doing no such thing. But it didn't matter. After that, calls from Helen got fewer and fewer. Finally, they stopped altogether."

Another social problem relates to age. The median age (50 percent above, 50 percent below) of widows is 69.7, while that of widowers is 71.7. This means that just at the time when they are grappling with grief and other emotional problems, they may also be feeling the real sting of being older and alone in a youth-worshipping society. Some widows discover to their amazement that their age, no matter what it is, is no deterrent to the husbands of some of their friends. Like the unmarried and divorced woman, they find they are considered by some men as "fair game—in need of servicing," as one widow put it.

For these and the psychological reasons having to do with bereavement, widows are slower to date again than divorced women. Widowed men seem to get back into the swim sooner, if not easier, than widowed women, and they seem to enjoy a slight edge where invitations are concerned, but not much. They, too, complain of being dropped by married friends.

Paradoxically, it is widows rather than widowers who begin to enjoy singlehood once they get into it. In "Challenge" workshops many more widowed women than men say they do not want to get married again. These women say they have come to relish their freedom and independence, even preferring not to live with their married children.

In fact, in a recent study of widowed women by sociologist Helena Lopata, a full 90 percent of the widows did not live with their married children because they preferred to live alone. Widowed men, on the other hand, experience the loss of their mates not only as a personal crisis, but as a domestic one as well—involving housework, laundry, marketing, cooking, and possibly child care. For widowers with children, a major problem is financial. The average wife is not covered by sufficient life insurance to pay for the services of a housekeeper for very long. It is scarcely any wonder that more widowed men than women jump back into marriage, and they do it sooner, too.

Unless the widow has a special source of income, finances are sure to be a problem for her too, no matter what her age. While the younger widow may be more physically able to work than the older widow and more likely to find jobs, she is more likely to have children to care for. Unless they have been working right along, widows of all ages complain about the difficulties of finding really interesting positions and of making enough money when they do.

Until recently, the widowed—like other singles—were strictly on their own as far as society was concerned. Now, there are a few services which address themselves specifically to this group. Self-help widow-to-widow programs were started in Boston and Houston last year and seem to be spreading to other parts of the country. These are organizations of widow volunteers who are willing to give of their time, understanding, and experience to help other widows.

In New York, a Widows' Consultation Center, started three years ago, provides psychiatric consultation, legal advice, and social activities with other widows. These services are available for a small fee.

Before the widowed can really get on with the business of living their lives, they have to come to grips with the psychological problems we discussed earlier. They may be held back from dating or starting relationships out of a sense of loyalty to the departed spouse—or out of a sense of self-pity or social awkwardness in their new role as a single. But their biggest problem is having to make so many new beginnings and cope with so many pressing practical and financial matters at the very time they are trying to get their feelings in order. Widowed men and women need all the help they can muster in getting through the "grief work" and solving their practical problems, but they will have to do most of the important work themselves.

THE SINGLE MOTHER AND THE WEEKEND FATHER

In talking with singles who have youngsters, we have noted a wide variety of attitudes and feelings toward their role as a single parent. In thinking about the phrase "single parent," one usually assumes it to be the mother who, through death or divorce, has moved into the new role of head of the household.

It is true that about 90 percent of children in single-parent households do live with their mothers as a result of death or divorce. There is also a growing number of singles who are parents by choice, usually through adoption or because of accidental conception and a decision to go through with the pregnancy even though marriage with the baby's father is not likely (or not desired). In some cases women deliberately become pregnant without letting the father know of the situation. Carole Klein's book *The Single Parent Experience* deals with this situation in some depth.

Most of the literature in this area deals almost entirely with the single mother—and that is understandable, considering the multitude of problems she faces in raising her children alone. But there is another, little discussed, side to that picture, and it concerns divorced fathers, 90 percent of whom do *not* have custody of their children and finally become what might be called forgotten parents.

Although many fathers, once divorced, seem to take little interest in their children (the average duration of child-support payment is around 14 months), there are many fathers who do care deeply about their children and feel an enormous sense of loss. Such single fathers say they suffer most from the emotional sparsity of being a Saturday or weekend parent, of feeling left out and isolated from children they love and want to be with.

Bill described his experience as a single parent this way: "My divorce was a fairly amicable one. My wife and I both agreed that I would support her and our young children, since she preferred staying home to look after them rather than going back to work. But what has happened is that I've become a weekend father and sometimes only a Saturday father. It is not because I want it that way, but it's what often happens after a divorce. My ex-wife and I quarrel constantly when we're together—more than we did before the divorce, and that's no good for the kids. But Lord how I miss them through the week. I once saw them seven days a week—now I only see them for two days or not at all if I have to be out of town. I really love those kids, and it just tears me apart when I have to say goodbye to them."

Bill's experience is a common problem—and one of which the rest of the population has little knowledge. On the positive side, though it's admittedly small comfort, single fathers often mention that the quality of the time they spend with their children seems to be greatly enhanced. They are able to plan their time better and give the children fuller attention—something frequently lacking in marriage.

Single-parent mothers don't have the same problem as their ex-mates, but as they will tell you, they have just about everything else. Usually their feelings are mixed. They are frequently angry at having to be both mother and father and bearing full responsibility for the children at all times, usually without enough money, which makes it an even greater chore. On the other hand, they often feel a great sense of relief that they are finally the only one to make decisions on how they will bring up their children and can do things their own way.

Most of them, like Marianne, complain of the great difficulty in trying to have a social life. "I work all day," she says, "and then when I start getting dressed for a dinner date and have to leave my four-year-old with a sitter after I've already been gone all day, I feel so selfish and so guilty, especially if he starts crying as I go out the door." When you realize how painful this is even for married mothers who work, you can understand how much more difficult it can be for a single working mother.

Writing in *Momma* (a new tabloid published in Los Angeles and addressed to the 7 million to 11 million single mothers in the United States with children under 18), a young woman expressed her hopes as a single mother: "I want responsible work, lots of friends for me and my daughter, mobility, enough money, a nice place to live, a good place for my daughter to spend her days, leisure time." How does the single mother feel? She writes, "Alone, tired, responsible, overworked, pleased, afraid, hilarious, touched, progressing, angry, hopeful, 'on top of it.'" Much of it sounds a little grim, but there's a hopeful note.

These difficulties of being a single parent are hardly news to anyone. They have been much discussed, documented, and dramatized. What are frequently overlooked, however, are the many advantages—to both you and your child—in being a single parent.

As in all things about the single, mythology abounds, but look at the facts. Although most single parents have a sense of guilt at not providing a father or a mother for their child, numerous studies by social scientists should provide the comforting knowledge that children in these circumstances are probably not suffering as much as we are sometimes led to believe.

Psychologists like Dr. William F. Reynolds, of Queens College in New York, have shown that children of divorced parents suffer less from emotional and physical problems than children living in a two-parent home where there is much marital conflict. In addition, because there is one less opinion to be reckoned with, there is more tranquility and stability in the home. And this is hardly an isolated study. Almost every scientific investigation in recent years has concluded that most youngsters of divorce turn out emotionally sounder than those living in the discord of a bad marriage.

An older divorced woman was telling a younger divorcée with children about this in a singles workshop. "My biggest worry when I was raising my son alone was that he would grow up spoiled, bitter and unhappy—but it didn't happen that way. After the first year of adjustment, we were a happier family than before. My son has been successful in his life and career, and all my old fears didn't come to pass."

Some single parents have even pointed out that one of the advantages to the single parent of having a child is the very fact that raising a child gives a certain amount of direction to one's life and may alleviate, in part, the problems of loneliness.

One of the best self-help organizations is Parents Without Partners; we highly recommend it. It is made up of single parents who are bringing up children alone. Its monthly magazine, *The Single Parent,* has articles and information of interest to the single parent, from financial problems to dating, and contains reviews of the latest books and magazines relating to the single parent. If you live in a metropolitan area you will probably find the address and phone number of Parents Without Partners in your telephone directory.

CAMARADERIE—ONE NEED NOT BE AN ODD NUMBER

By now, you, as a single—reading here about the common problems and difficulties of the divorced, widowed, and separated—may be absorbing some of the sense of camaraderie all singles begin to discover in "Challenge" workshops. Probably you, too, are now sharing a sense of that overlap of experience and feeling that binds all singles together once they have a chance to compare notes—no matter what their personality, age, or background. And it is this common thread—the sharing of the single experience—that is the core of what we have called the singles community.

On the face of it, the widowed, divorced, and separated have a great deal in common. They have all been through what is often a searing experience that leaves its "victim" isolated and shocked at the sudden necessity of moving from one state of life to another.

In fact, Dr. Thomas Holmes, a University of Washington psychiatrist, found that the most stressful life events on his "social readjustment scale" were (1) death of a spouse, (2) a divorce, and (3) a marital separation. These events often lead to major illnesses and are found to be more stressful than such traumatic occurrences as the death of a close family member or even a long jail term.

So it might seem that the widowed, divorced, and separated

would have a very clear, intuitive understanding of their common needs and problems. But this doesn't prove to be the case. However, once they get together and talk about it all, the insight of the commonly felt pain comes through to them, and they greet one another as long-lost friends.

This is in no small measure due to the never-marrieds, who know about the problems of singleness all too well. After all, they have been coping with singleness all their lives. In the give and take, the never-marrieds discover they have a lot to give—of time-tested ideas and experiences in dealing with the problems, feelings, and inequities of being single.

And it is hardly a one-way street. The never-marrieds get the benefit of some hard, realistic thinking about marriage from the best experts in the world—people who have been there. They usually end up becoming more aware of their many freedoms and feeling better about being single.

The widowed, divorced, and separated, in turn, feel that somebody at last cares about them and really understands them, as they listen to the never-marrieds and to each other. They start sharing experiences and making friends with other singles, often for the first time. At long last, they discover that "one" need not be an odd number.

4. Alone
—But Not Lonely

If you ask most singles what aspect of their life they most dislike, or what they fear most about being single, they will usually answer, "loneliness." If you ask further whether they really fear being alone, which need not mean loneliness at all, the answer comes with less certainty. In society the distinction between the two is so rarely made that loneliness and being alone are confused with each other. And the fear of being alone, i.e., lonely, is so great that it propels many people into marriage without their even recognizing what is motivating them.

Briefly, loneliness can be defined as an acute longing for companionship, a feeling of bleakness, of isolation, and of being cut off from others in an uncomfortable, even despairing way. Being alone, on the other hand, means simply being by one's self. It can make you miserable—if you can only see it in terms of loneliness—or it can be quite enjoyable, a source of infinite possibilities once you appreciate the positive uses of being by yourself.

No one can deny the reality of loneliness—it certainly exists; and being alone, which must be accepted as a basic part of the single life, is certainly a stimulant to it. But contrary to popular opinion, it can eventually prove most rewarding, for we can learn to turn loneliness into being alone, and to appreciate the value of being alone and turn it to our advantage. Before we can do this, though, we need to understand what it is. In our fast-paced civilization, we often are so busy running away in panic from loneliness that we never take the time to figure out what it is about it that terrifies us so.

The first barrier standing in the way of any analysis is the emotional content that has been loaded into the word "loneliness." Society views loneliness primarily, if not entirely, as negative, bad, or debilitating, something to be rid of and forgotten as quickly as possible. How many times have you told a friend who asked how you were that you were "lonely," if that was how you felt at the moment? If you were angry, you would say "angry." If you were happy, you would say "happy," but if you were lonely, you might well evade the whole subject by replying: "Under the weather," "Okay, I guess," or just plain "Ugh"—anything but confess you were lonely.

Loneliness, to many people, connotes failure, rejection, or not being pretty enough, bright enough, or desirable enough to warrant the company of another. In our society we see ourselves so much in terms of how others see us that when no one is around to validate our existence we almost feel that we don't exist. Is it any surprise then that we are afraid of loneliness? Without a doubt it is a bad word. And the lack of communication about loneliness increases the terror that it holds for many of us and inevitably makes one feel that other people do not experience it with similar distress.

LONELINESS—IT HAPPENS TO EVERYONE

Loneliness can overwhelm anyone, even in the company of others. It can happen at a party or public gathering—and at such times it can be even more poignant because one is not supposed to feel lonely then. Being surrounded by other people is supposed to take away loneliness. Indeed, it can and often does, but only if you have learned how to deal with loneliness. If you have spent most of your life running away from it rather than facing it, neither being alone nor being with people will work for you.

We know many people—and you probably know some yourself—who have demonstrated time and again that being alone need not involve the feelings of isolation and negativism associated with loneliness. As you might have guessed, we have found that it is purely an adjustment in their attitudes that allows these people to do it. Most importantly, it is a state of mind that can be learned simply by living through those periods of loneliness with greater and greater awareness, with more and more success, until finally you come to realize that these experiences are themselves a great source of strength for you. Being alone then begins to look more and more like an opportunity to grow, a time to be used for enhancing your life, a kind of haven for sorting out ideas and plans, a quiet time for decision making, for doing the things you really want to do, and for planning for the days ahead.

It took Barry about a year after his divorce before he could begin to see being alone this way: "During those first three or four months after my divorce I thought I'd go batty. No wife and kids to greet me when I came home from work. I'd walk into my tomb-quiet apartment, and the silence nearly killed me. The first thing I would do was turn on the radio to a talk show so I could hear someone else's voice. I even started talking to myself to keep from feeling so lonely. But it's different now, especially when I've had an exhausting day at the office wrangling with a bunch of people. I actually look forward to the peace and quiet when I come home. To me, being alone no longer means being lonely."

The change in Barry's outlook was accomplished by something no more complicated than just surviving what he now calls, with some pride, his "blue period." We have known many others like Barry who, having come out of similar long periods of trial, now look back on them with greater self-assurance, as if they were decorated veterans of a far-off battle campaign. It is a kind of pride that is well justified; one might even say it is one well worth earning.

Judging by the treatment of the subject in the popular press, one might suspect that loneliness was a newly discovered disease, an outgrowth of what is called alienation, but the truth is that it is a basic and time-honored part of what is commonly called the human condition. Loneliness has been around a long time, and though it may not be possible to overcome it, you can overcome your fear of it, and in doing so, change it into something of value.

FACING IT

The Indian philosopher Krishnamurti said, "When you are willing to face what *is,* then the loneliness comes to an end because it is completely transformed." For Krishnamurti what "is," is the loneliness itself. Facing loneliness means understanding what it means to you and pinpointing some of the specific things that trigger it for you. In order to help master it, try practicing two very simple techniques.

Accepting It

First, and most important, is the strategy of acceptance. It is necessary not to try to escape from loneliness when it hits you. The possible escapes include alcohol, overeating, drugs, constant TV watching, constant work, frenzied activities of every kind, particularly exhaustive attempts at fun, and having someone—anyone—around all the time. These escapes will, in the long run, only make the pangs of loneliness more intense when those hours come, as they inevitably do, when you are truly physically alone—when you wake up at 2 A.M., for example, in a mood as dark as the room around you. It is at times like these, when no one else is around, that you must face *you* and there is simply no escaping it. But the trick is not to let things get to this crisis point if you can help it. And the way to do that is not to get into the habit of escape.

Escape has the effect of making the bill harder to pay when it finally comes due. Each time we go into one of our escape routines—and we all have many of them—our self-respect suffers just a bit. On the other hand, each time we practice acceptance, each time we simply say to ourselves, "OK, this is one of those times when I feel lonely. Let's see what I can get out of it," we gain in self-respect. Needless to say, it is those increments of self-respect that make the crises fewer and farther between and make them easier to get through when they happen.

A basic step in practicing acceptance of loneliness is to deliberately quiet the mind. Whatever else you may decide to do next—and we have specific suggestions later in this chapter—first sit quietly in a chair and try to get your feelings into perspective. Take some deep breaths, close your eyes, and try to come to the awareness that feeling lonely is okay, that it is a part of life, that everyone feels it at times—even married people. Instead of wallowing in loneliness or panick-

ing into the feeling that you must do something—anything—
to get rid of it, try thinking calmly about what loneliness
means to you, why you are afraid of it, and how you can use
it as a positive feature of your life.

Using It

The second technique follows naturally from the first. It
requires a little more positive commitment and a little more
determination. It is the strategy of putting loneliness to good
use. Yes, that is an old bromide; no, it is not an empty
platitude. After all, once you decide to accept the inevitability of a certain amount of loneliness, why not also decide
to turn those periods to your own advantage? They are the
times when you can most increase your feeling of self-
reliance, which is your most important asset as a single
person. And you will find that as you begin to perceive things
differently, you actually change what happens to you. If you
can begin to look upon such moments as self-learning and
growing times rather than simply dreary times to be suffered
through, you will find yourself gradually breaking through
any panic and self-pity into a kind of calm that may astound
you. Believe it is there—for it is.

At this point, we might ask why this whole subject of
loneliness, as universal to human experience as any other
emotional state one can name, causes such confusion,
despair, and helplessness? We believe, simply, that it is
because we lack the inner resources to be on our own.
Society relentlessly teaches us how to seek diversion and
entertainment, but it doesn't teach us how to nourish our
own selves or even to know our own selves. There is, as far as
we know, no self-knowledge or personal-growth industry to
match that devoted to entertainment in our culture. Lacking
the inner resources, we must turn to other individuals and

their experiences for help. In this chapter, the suggestions for accepting and using loneliness are based on the most successful that have come out of the "Challenge" workshops.

TRIGGERS TO LONELINESS

In learning to deal with loneliness, it helps to realize that there are specific times and situations in everyone's life which cause it. Understanding this can lessen the distress and dissipate much of the fear of loneliness, for when you know the conditions that result in such feelings, they will be more manageable when they occur.

There are hundreds of otherwise inconsequential events, places, and times of day, night, or year in the course of all our lives that may consistently provoke loneliness. Undoubtedly, single people suffer more on traditionally social Friday and Saturday nights, and generally on weekends, which is a time for being with a family and a time when one is free of many work-a-day distractions. A beautiful autumn day and no one to share it with, a rainy day when you can't go out, Christmas or Thanksgiving alone, birthdays, events that recall the past or mark the passages of time and create a sense of longing or nostalgia, any night when the house seems more quiet than usual, an old, familiar song, the sight of a couple walking arm in arm, a beautiful sunset—the list (a constant source of poetic inspiration) goes on and on, and many of the stimulants to loneliness appear to be universal.

While the following events happen less frequently in people's lives, when they do, they almost invariably trigger "attacks" of loneliness: the death of someone close or even their illness (at which time the prospect of death, normally kept well in the unconscious, surfaces); moving to a new city, new neighborhood, or new job; friends' moving away; traveling and finding yourself without familiar objects and distractions; retiring and finding one's whole life-style and sense of self changing drastically. Naturally, there are other times, too. When you are ill, fatigued, or depressed, or when you have suffered disappointments in your work or social life, your loneliness may be compounded by the fear that you are not making progress in your life and you therefore feel a certain sense of futility as well.

TECHNIQUES FOR DEALING WITH LONELINESS

We have been talking about the general circumstances that can trigger loneliness for most singles. The response to each stimulus varied greatly from person to person, and few may apply to you directly. But before you can deal with any loneliness, whatever its cause, you have to discover what it is that makes you lonely.

One way to do this is to keep a chart or journal of your feelings over a period of several weeks. By studying it and examining it for trends, you can begin to ask yourself some questions: When do I begin feeling lonely? What triggers it? How long does it last? Was I with a particular person when it began overtaking me? (Some people make us lonely.) Was I thinking about some past event or a person whom I miss?

Donna, a divorcée, after keeping a journal for six weeks, discovered her loneliest periods were when she was washing the dinner dishes after she had put her two small youngsters to bed. It dawned on her that this had been one of her best times when her marriage was good, but now that she was alone it had turned into her worst time. The source of the problem was that she had nothing in particular to look forward to. She solved it by having specific plans for each evening: reading a special book or magazine, having a friend in for dinner, taking a night class. With these specific plans, her loneliness went down the drain along with the dishwater.

The important thing is to take note of your loneliness when you sense it and to analyze exactly when it was that you started feeling it and what brought the loneliness on. Don't wait too long or you will forget what triggered the emotion. Incidentally, there are many advantages to such a journal, another one being that you will become more alert and perceptive about yourself in other ways as well. The keeping of diaries used to be far more common than it is today, and it was probably very valuable for the mental health and general sensitivity of the diarists. Today, in fact, it is part of the self-help techniques in use by some psychologists.

Once you discover what precipitates your loneliness, it isn't hard to figure out what to do about it. Very often, the simplest act—frequently one you have been postponing—can help alleviate these moments of distress.

□ A divorced man, finding that certain music evoked unhappy memories, gave away his half of the record collection he had inherited from his divorce.

□ A widow who had resisted getting rid of her husband's clothes and was still being reminded of him every time she walked into the closet a year after his death, finally gave them all to charity.

□ A divorcée finally traced her depressed breakfast feelings to a favorite oversized coffee mug that belonged to her ex-husband. Every time she saw it in the cupboard, she was reminded of her divorce. She broke it.

◻ A separated engineer discovered that going to his parent's house for Sunday dinner each week—a ritual he once faithfully performed with his wife—was making him lonely and nostalgic. Though it is more trouble, he now visits his parents on a week night, and saves Sunday for playing golf or tennis with friends.

By keeping a written record of his moods over a three-week period, Barry, whom we mentioned earlier, discovered that loneliness seemed to strike the minute he walked in the door of his apartment after a day in the office. "I finally pin-pointed what bothered me," he said. "It was the darkness—returning home to darkness. Also, the place looked bleak and dreary once I turned the lights on. So I painted the entrance hall a warm color and hung some of my favorite pictures there. Then I bought a lamp which I leave on when I go out. I find it makes all the difference in my mood. Environment always mattered to me. Now I even get up a few minutes earlier and straighten the front room so it will be more cheerful when I get home."

All the little things you can do to make your living quarters more friendly and warm will provide ammunition for combating loneliness. We should caution you, however, that there is a bull market nowadays on "tricks" for coping with loneliness. One guidebook for the single suggests: "It is harder to be lonely curled up cozily in a soft chair, supported by pink cushions, drinking tea out of a Wedgewood cup." Possibly, but one mustn't be too sure about it. Many singles, just because they expect material comfort to ease the discomfort of loneliness, are doubly disappointed when it doesn't.

Our surroundings can reflect the respect we have for ourselves and our contentment with the life we are living, or they can reflect our desire to escape into a fantasy of what we would like to be. The one environment will help us to be happy; the other is sure to make us feel more lonely.

The experience of Susie, a thirty-eight-year-old divorcée, is a good example of how material possessions don't cure loneliness. Susie decided she was going to be a chic divorcée in a big way when she was divorced. She bought a new wardrobe and had a friend with designing talent help her decorate her new four-room apartment. After the shag rug, the glass-and-chrome table, the potted plants, and the abstract paintings were all in place, she settled down to feel great—only that wasn't how she felt. "I had the image, but I didn't have the inner tranquility I needed to live up to it," she said later. "At first, when I was upset, I would run out to buy something else for the apartment or myself—a new pillow or a new dress—but nothing worked. Finally, I realized the work I had to do was on myself."

There is a subtle but telling difference between the approach taken by Barry and Susie. We would submit that Barry's was successful because he calmly took stock of his situation, analyzed his feelings, isolated what was bothering him, and then invested some positive emotional energy to correct it. It became, therefore, a labor of self-love; it was not an exercise in glossing over his surroundings with the trappings of comfort. And from "Challenge" workshops, there are many other examples of how singles have found "solutions" to loneliness, once they understood its nature.

Tim, a thirty-one-year-old never-married dentist, was one of these. He thought he was enjoying his social whirl. He gave dinners and parties, was invited to many others, and was constantly on the go. After one particularly lively Saturday night party, he woke up the next day feeling miserable. He decided, for the first time in years, to spend the day alone. Sitting quietly and thinking about his life, he suddenly came to a startling discovery: he wasn't really getting that much enjoyment out of all his socializing.

He also realized he was feeling lonely, desperately lonely, and he had a great urge to talk to someone about it. Thinking of the people he knew, he made a second startling discovery: his contacts were basically superficial, and there wasn't a single person he felt he could talk to openly and honestly. As a result of this short bout of soul-searching, Tim decided to change the way he was living. He eliminated all parties except those he truly wanted to go to; he started exploring courses at a university extension in subjects that intrigued him but he had never taken time to pursue; and he started looking for—and finding—new friends with whom he could have deeper relationships. He also found that for the first time in his life he was able to be alone and enjoy himself.

Analyzing your loneliness and figuring out when it seems to happen to you is no guarantee that it will not occur again. But each time it does, if you will face your loneliness and accept it, it will pain you less and less.

None of these discoveries and actions will keep you from being lonely at times, but they may help you avoid being consistently pushed into a negative emotional state and then wondering why.

There are some things you can do positively when you have accepted loneliness. All demand a certain amount of purposeful activity (not escapism) as opposed to passivity, which only intensifies feelings of isolation. They are certainly more trouble than watching TV, but they work.

Talk to Someone Who Cares

Have a telephone "hot-line" list, written or in your head, of the people that have the kind of empathy for you and your problems that can "lift" you when you're lonely. Perhaps all your friends know how to listen sympathetically and provide the emotional support we all need, but usually there will be one or two special people who do this best.

Evelyn and Rod, both newly divorced, in their early forties and long-time friends, worked out a hot-line buddy arrangement for "anytime loneliness might get one of us down." Evelyn called Rod about the new job she had her heart set on getting that went to somebody else. She took the news in her stride during the day, but about eleven that night, she suddenly felt dejected and lonely. She called Rod, as they had agreed they would do whenever either of them was depressed, and he provided her with the emotional boost she needed. Rod called Evelyn when he got a call from his ex-wife one night telling him she was remarrying. They vouch that the system works.

The phone may seem too impersonal an instrument to convey your feelings at such sensitive times, and obviously, being with someone who cares is better, but the point is to actively do something with someone in your own behalf.

Do Something Physical

Take a vigorous walk, bicycle, job, go to a gym, exercise, practice yoga, or scrub the floor. William Ball, director of the American Conservatory Theater in San Francisco, who uses meditation along with other psychological techniques in drawing the best from his actors, observes that "it is impossible to feel happy if the body is draggy and depressed." He concludes from this, for both actors and people in real life:

"We must *do* the act, and the feeling will follow." The link between the body and the mind is a strong one. Some people's sense of emotional well-being is immensely enhanced by physical activity. And just as we can use our minds to monitor or control physical pain, so we can use deliberately calculated body movements of freedom and joy to ease the strains and stresses of our mind. It works both ways.

Do Something You've Been Wanting to Do

It may be as simple as going to an art gallery or the museum. Go shopping. You don't have to buy anything—just browse. It is a more active version of what the Italians call *dolce farniente* (sweet nothing-to-do) and works wonders on feelings of loneliness, for men as well as women.

It is well known that a deliberate change of scene spirits you out of your mood before you even know it's happening. This was the idea behind the grand tour or the sea-change of an ocean voyage recommended for curing depression in Victorian times. Remember that you are not fleeing from yourself or your loneliness—you are accepting the opportunity to be alone and not in communication with others, in order to get into communication with yourself. You have to bestir yourself. No one else can do it for you. Put on your coat, turn out the lights (or leave them on), and go!

Change Your Inner Pace

Get down to reading some books or articles you have been wanting to tackle for ages. Again, the idea is not to divert attention but to fill your life by fulfilling your own desires. Enjoy being alone for what it is—free time to do what you want.

One widower keeps a list of books he wants to read in his

wallet. If he is feeling lonely, he either buys a book on the list or gets it from a library. Repeatedly, he finds that the anticipation of reading something he has wanted to read is enough to jog him out of his mood. Anticipation is half the pleasure, so prepare yourself. Be ready to have a good time by yourself.

Do Something for Someone Else

It may sound Pollyanna-ish to say that the more we help others, the more we forget about ourselves, but it has always worked and it will work for you. There is such a need for simple human compassion in this world, just listening intently to a friend's troubles (as he or she has listened to yours) is probably the greatest thing we can do for someone we like. Try it and see how it lessens your own isolation.

Plan Ahead

Make plans for evenings and weekends, especially, and for trips and vacations, too. Some singles hate to be held down by schedules, plans, or obligations. Until they get rid of this notion, they are not likely to appreciate the many pleasures of planning ahead. But once they start planning, they will probably agree that pleasures are indeed doubled in this way, for one feels in control of one's destiny. Planning for a trip by learning the language or more about the country, or preparing a wardrobe, can enhance the enjoyment of the actual travel.

Christmas holidays can be particularly trying and lonely for singles without close family ties. They can seem heart-rending for the newly divorced or widowed, especially those with small children. Suzanne solved it by inviting several singles—with and without children—to spend her first Christmas as a divorcée with her and her six- and eight-year-old sons. Everyone brought some food, and what might have been a time of painful loneliness was turned into a festive and happy occasion by a little advance thought and planning.

Keep a Scrapbook

It may seem ridiculously simple, but people have always been inspired by homilies, poems, or advice that is meaningful to them. In a sense, this is like having a friend close by at all times ready to help you, but it's especially helpful when you're feeling lonely and you need to remember the wisdom and guidelines that helped before.

A single man we know, who keeps all his inspirational quotes and clippings in a hard-back notebook, calls it his "K-ration"—a term used in World War II for a packet of concentrated food to be used in survival situations. Another man framed a short relevant article from a newspaper and hung it beside his desk for a quick pick-me-up whenever he was feeling depressed.

GETTING THROUGH IT

Many creative thinkers who have learned to live with and trust their feelings have discovered that there is no way out of loneliness but through it. For them, especially, it becomes important not to turn away, out of fear, from the full experience of loneliness, knowing that on the other side of the tunnel they will find the "truths" they are seeking. Most poets and novelists, notoriously solitary workers, are keenly aware of these uses of loneliness in prying open the mind and enlarging vision and creative energy. They know that loneliness can be a source of spiritual, intellectual, and artistic growth. Thomas Wolfe said: "The whole conviction of my life now rests upon the belief that loneliness, far from being a rare and curious phenomenon, peculiar to myself and to a few other solitary men, is the central and inevitable fact of human existence. Loneliness is an essential condition of creativity." Although very few of us have the talent for significant creative work (or are using it if we do), there is no reason to feel that we cannot create on our own level. The product of that creativity, even if meaningful only to ourselves, is well worth making the effort for.

The basic way out of your loneliness, then, is not to go around it or climb over it, not to escape from it or bottle it up in an effort to hide its existence, but to face it squarely—analyzing it, understanding it, cultivating it (if necessary, softening its blow), and finally making it your friend. To help you do this, you might try what one single did in a workshop session as she was grappling with the problem. She took the phrase "I am lonesome," deleted the "l" from "lonesome," and transposed the remaining letters to read, "someone." Result: "I am someone." And remember too—just as it is okay to be single (or alone), it is okay to be lonely too.

When loneliness can be transformed in this way into a comfortable state of being alone, then going out alone, the subject of our next chapter, can change from a source of dread into one of pleasant anticipation.

5. Going Out Alone and Traveling Alone

The opportunity to go out alone is potentially one of the most rewarding experiences of the single life. If you don't agree with that statement, this chapter is for you.

"Why even talk about going out alone?" asked a young never-married man in a "Challenge" workshop. "It's no problem. You just open the door and out you go."

"That's what you think," shot back a thirty-seven-year-old recent divorcée. "I handle all kinds of important tasks in my job but I'd rather draw up and present a complicated annual report than go to a social gathering by myself."

"That's right," affirmed an engineer in his late forties. "After my wife died, I felt that way just walking into the first meeting or two of a community college evening class in human relations. I was so conscious of being alone, you would have thought I was a callow schoolboy. It's not so easy when you are used to doing everything in tandem."

For some singles—particularly the never-married—it is the

easiest, most natural thing in the world; while for others—especially those who enter the single world after having been married for a long time—going out alone is one of the most difficult and depressing aspects of being single.

The difficulty can be traced to a mixed bag of feelings, notably embarrassment, fear, and frustration—all of which result from the central fact of life that out there, it's a paired world. Almost anyone who has ever gone out alone knows something of what it feels like—especially if you have gone to a party by yourself and found that you were standing alone in a corner while everyone else was laughing and chatting in couples or groups. At such a time, who hasn't had thoughts like these: How did I ever get in a situation like this? Where do I go to hide? What do I do now? Maybe I should turn around and walk out! I'll never go out alone again! If this kind of distress is an approximation of your feelings in social situations, the problem may not be so much with your social skills as with your expectations of what your social life should be.

For those of you who don't go out alone or don't go out as often as you would like, or don't enjoy it when you do go out, this chapter will present some hints, suggestions, and ideas—tools, if you will—that other singles have used to turn going out alone into a positive experience. But, first, it is necessary to analyze some of the psychological reasons why this aspect of the single life presents such a problem for so many people.

WHY DON'T YOU GO OUT ALONE?

The reasons singles give themselves and others for not going out alone are usually not the real ones. Instead, they are excuses for not dealing with a variety of psychological problems—problems from which we all suffer at times, but which seem to particularly afflict the single because of our social training. It is easy to say, "I'm tired at the end of the day," or "I have too much to do," or "There's a special TV program I want to see," or "I'm afraid to go out alone at night" (the cry of many people in urban areas). Of course, there are times when any of these may be true, but we are talking about those other occasions—when you want to go out but you cannot bring yourself to make the effort required. We can state, with virtual certainty, that what really is holding you back is not those platitudes but your attitudes:

Embarrassment

A great many singles complain that they feel just plain embarrassed when they are alone. Simply "being seen in public" triggers this. No one knows if you're alone at home, but in public, why, that's another story. Singles feel they are being stared at by other people and viewed as social failures, even by strangers, because they are not with someone. This may sound somewhat paranoid, but it is an accurate description of the way many single people feel, even though they are aware that their feelings are an exaggeration of the truth of the situation. Social changes may well be taking place, but women particularly feel themselves being judged as losers when they are not accompanied by men. Or a woman may be embarrassed that other people—especially men—might think she is looking for a "pick-up" when she ventures out alone. She may be additionally distressed at the prospects of then having to fend off unwanted advances.

People do frequently cast curious glances in theaters or restaurants, and there are many other ways in which society conspires to let you know you are out of line when you are alone. On the other hand, all the feelings of embarrassment we have mentioned depend directly on one's own negative inner feelings about being single. If you work on changing these negative feelings, which this chapter (indeed, this whole book) intends to help you do, eventually how you feel about yourself will become more important to you than what you imagine others think about you.

Limited Social Confidence

For some single men and women, fear of going out alone may grow out of a conviction that they are deficient in social skills. And they may very well be inexperienced at exercising many of them—especially newly divorced or widowed singles, who are used to relating socially as part of a couple. For them, it is often quite difficult to make the adjustment to being fully confident on their own. They may feel so awkward around others that they stay home and avoid the problem entirely.

Even for singles who are accustomed to being on their own, going alone to parties, dances, or other gatherings activates the fear of actually being rejected by somebody. This is not a totally unrealistic fear. No matter how skillful one is socially, the sheer unpredictability of other people makes it nearly impossible to know in advance precisely how a social situation will turn out. More often than not, people are receptive to one another, but the occasional experience of the cold shoulder or withering remark painfully lingers in one's memory. Thus, many people prefer the security of their familiar surroundings at home to the risk of new adventures, no matter how potentially rewarding.

Fear of Further Disappointment

When you go out alone, the motive must be your own enjoyment of the particular thing you are doing—and this must be held clearly in mind—otherwise you may easily fall into a frustration and disappointment trap. The mechanism works this way: If your real motive in going out is the old search for the one-and-only, you are certain to (1) fail to find him or her, (2) not have a good time, and (3) wind up feeling like a failure. You will have wasted your time, and you will be frustrated. In a country with an intense romantic tradition like ours, not to have found one's great romance can be experienced as the ultimate personal defeat. And each time you go out on the search you relive that ultimate defeat. The real danger is that reliving defeat over and over again can lead to a general despair which will keep you from wanting to go out alone for any purpose—just stepping out the door can come to be a painful reminder of one's failure. So some disenchanted singles hide away at home, not daring to risk another disappointment.

These attitudes are understandable and deserving of sympathy. They are also wrong. Once any of these stay-at-home singles have broken through their fears and had a taste of the advantages of going out alone, such negative patterns often change with surprising abruptness.

THE ADVANTAGES OF GOING OUT ALONE

In conversations with singles who have positive attitudes about going out alone, the same advantages are named over and over again—the unique benefits of the single situation.

Coming and Going When You Want To
Marrieds seldom can go anywhere or do anything in their free time without either consulting their spouses or going as a twosome. As a single, you have the opportunity to enjoy the exhilaration of making your own choices.

Listen to Mary, a twenty-four-year-old never-married:

"When I first moved to Los Angeles and my date would say, 'Why not meet me at such-and-such a party?' I used to get downright offended. 'How come he doesn't pick me up in his car?' I'd ask myself. My boyfriends in Cleveland always did. But then I'd usually go ahead and meet him there. Of course, the distances in Los Angeles are horrendous, but I was still kind of hurt. Gradually I got used to the idea of either going to a party by myself or arranging to meet someone there.

"One night, I went out for the first time with a guy who really turned out to be quite an unpleasant person. We had come in separate cars, luckily. When he got into an argument at the party and started creating a bad scene, I simply got in my car and left. Since then, I go everywhere alone, if possible. I've come to enjoy that lovely feeling of being in control of where I want to be."

Meeting People without Restrictions

A person alone is far more likely to meet someone new (of the same or opposite sex) than one who is already paired and has the obligation to stay with the person with whom he or she came. At first glance, it may seem that we're copping out on the subject of this section—the advantages of going out alone—but note that we're listing this as an *advantage* and not the *purpose* of going out alone. We certainly don't advise habitual outings just to find someone; but obviously a new friend is a possible result of any encounter. This subtle difference in intent can add greatly to your pleasure if an encounter happens and will save you from disappointment when one doesn't.

Deciding to Go Somewhere on a Moment's Notice

Since you, as a single, don't have to make plans and you don't have to ask, consider, or tell anyone else, you increase your potential for adventures.

Joe, a thirty-five-year-old divorced man, told a group of

singles what he saw as the main pleasure of his new single life: "It's freedom," he said. "It's that wonderful feeling of not having to account for your minutes and your hours all the time, like you were some kind of child and your wife was your mother. Oh, I know women don't like to be nags either, but these are easy roles to fall into when you're married. And if you like being independent, it's a hard cross to bear.

"Last Sunday morning, on the spur of the moment, I went to a yoga class I had read about in the newspaper. Then, when some others were going to a brunch at a neighbor's and asked me along, I went. Later we went bowling. I got home about six after an extraordinarily delightful and spontaneous day. That's the kind of freedom I want in my life."

Pursuing Your Own Interests and Bypassing Things That You Don't Want to Do

Many divorced and widowed people, in thinking back to their marriages, say they gave up going to or doing what they wanted early in the game. In an effort to please a spouse who didn't share their interests, they didn't pursue any of them for years and had almost forgotten what they were.

Before his divorce, Seth felt guilty every time he played tennis because his wife hated the sport and wouldn't join him. After his divorce, he took it up again, and it has become a source of real pleasure in his life.

Mary loved going to foreign films; her husband didn't like movies at all. Rather than nag or go alone (even married people suffer from the hate-going-out-alone syndrome!), she gave up seeing them entirely. One of the pleasures of being divorced, she says, is going out to dinner and spending a leisurely evening at the movies—all alone—seeing whatever she pleases.

This freedom to be yourself and follow your own interests seems to be so important to people that many marriages have floundered because of the lack of it. In fact, the idea of separate vacations, which some couples prefer, seems to represent an effort to introduce some of the single life into the coupled state.

What all these advantages of going out alone have in common is a chance to exercise one's freedom to cultivate and practice an adventurous spirit. Some people find this attitude easier to acquire on trips, but it should be part of your everyday single life. You don't have to be away on vacation, far removed from your home territory, to make setting out alone a positive experience. The same adventurous spirit that stimulates and propels you in a foreign country can be equally valuable when you set out alone to the local art gallery, museum of natural history, zoo, adult education course, or local bistro.

EATING OUT ALONE

People in "Challenge" workshops often remark that one of the most troublesome aspects of going out by yourself is eating alone.

Typical is the never-married bachelor of forty-seven who was asked why he never protested if he was given a table he didn't like while dining alone in a restaurant (in case you haven't noticed, all tables with a magnificent view of the kitchen's swinging doors seem to be reserved for singles). He answered, "I guess I just don't have the guts. I know it's hard to understand, especially if you're married, but eating alone in a nice restaurant is the one thing that probably bugs me most about being single. And if it bothers me this much, I can imagine how much it bothers some single women."

A married actress told a group of singles that the first time she really understood what singles were up against as a group was during a tour in an Eastern city. She had gone into a restaurant alone and after standing there for more than a few minutes waiting to be noticed was finally asked the classic question by the maitre d'.

"Two?" he said imperiously, as if hoping that she had a man hiding behind her. "No, just me," she blurted, a little nonplussed, "I'm alone." "Come," he said, "I'll hide you over here at one end of these tables on the side." He pointed to a remote wing of tables, and she got the picture instantly. "No," she said firmly. "As a matter of fact, I don't want to hide. How about one of these in the center of the room?" "I'm sorry, these are reserved," he answered. "Well, kindly unreserve one for me," she said. "I want the light where I can study a script." "We wouldn't want you to be seen alone," he responded solicitously, and it took a little further persuasion on her part before he gave her a table that would expose her oneness.

Most singles report a mixture of emotions when they are asked, "Are you alone?" in the better restaurants, as if it weren't perfectly obvious that they were. The experience is insulting, discouraging, and infuriating. At the very least, it puts you on the defensive and can take the edge off both your enjoyment of your night out and your appetite. One way to handle this particular problem is to prevent it from occurring. One woman did this by quickly saying, when she was approached by the maitre d', "I'm alone and I'd like a good table for one, please." This makes the question unnecessary and keeps you off the defensive. That imperious, "Are you alone?" has done more to frighten singles away from good eating places than all the high prices in the world.

During her marriage, Joan had hated marketing and cooking, and ate out almost every night with her husband. The arrangement seemed convenient, until her husband announced that he wanted a divorce (and presumably a home-cooked dinner). Joan was upset but, as she surveyed her future, one of the main things that distressed her was the prospect of having to give up eating in restaurants.

With the advice of some friends, however, she gradually worked out a scheme for doing it. She chose a neighborhood restaurant, asked for a table for two, saying a companion might be joining her, waited a while as she read a book, then ordered, ate her dinner, and left. The first few times were excruciating. But as she pursued the plan at other, fancier restaurants, she finally gained enough poise and assurance to give up the subterfuges—reading a book and saying that someone might join her. Instead, she sat contentedly, thoroughly enjoying her dinner and chatting with the waiters.

Direct action, then, seems to be the antidote to being treated as a second-class citizen in restaurants. Here is a simple, three-point plan that combines techniques worked out by many singles.

(1) Cultivate a few restaurants consistently until you become one of their favored, regular customers, and it no longer matters to them that you are alone. Naturally, all restaurants would rather sell two meals than one, but a single steady customer is worth a number of couples who come infrequently.

(2) Get to know all the waiters by name, even the proprietor and cook. This not only guarantees that you can always get a table, but it often results in having special dishes prepared the way you want.

In exchange for the good treatment you receive, recommend your restaurant to your friends and be sure they tell the headwaiter you sent them. This will make the whole arrangement homier, and your "home away from home" can provide a special sense of belonging that is very pleasant for the single.

(3) Show little courtesies, like going early before the crowds, calling for a reservation before you go, and not lingering when you are through if the place is crowded. And remember that a consistently good but not exaggerated tip is more appreciated than occasional splurges.

Once you start putting these suggestions to work, not only will you soon find that eating out becomes easier, but you will feel a positive enjoyment in doing it.

Some singles feel that going to such elaborate lengths to ensure such fair treatment by a good restaurant is in some way "pandering." We feel rather that it is merely recognizing some facts of life: Good restaurants are busy, and they get most of their business from couples. Coming earlier usually improves your chances of getting a good table whether you are married or single, and lingering, even if you are a couple, is not a fair practice during the rush hour.

Realism would seem to require acknowledging these few facts, while reserving for yourself the right to present yourself as a first-class customer with the full expectation of being treated as such. But once that happens, don't let success blind you to a minor little satisfaction which one single says is the best part of eating out alone for him. It may be for you, too. He is a stockbroker and takes some of his market reports to dinner with him—to read.

"Who says it isn't polite to read when you eat?" he asks. "It isn't mentioned in Emily Post—or anywhere else, in fact. It is one of my chief joys, actually—especially when I can find a restaurant that has enough light. I sit there, plow through my reading, get a lot of work done, and enjoy it. You would be surprised at the number of couples—and singles too—who watch me enviously."

TRAVELING ALONE

If eating alone in a restaurant takes a certain amount of courage for the uninitiated, traveling alone takes even more, and staying a week or two alone somewhere takes more than that. As with eating out alone, this problem is more severe for women, but it affects many men as well. Because it involves more planning, traveling alone is a greater investment of time, money, energy. Therefore, the potential rewards are greater—for enjoyment, learning, and personal growth.

Until they have tried it, most singles seem to dread the idea of traveling alone. And they avoid it for the same reasons they hang back from going out alone anywhere— particularly fear of embarrassment or rejection. Once you've tried it, however, you may become a travel-alone devotee much more quickly than you think. It is the experience itself that converts the fear of the unknown into a real adventure *into* the unknown. The more you travel, the more you find that you enjoy whatever happens, no matter what happens.

Your primary motive in traveling should be to pursue your own interests and enjoy yourself. Anyone you meet on a trip should be appreciated as an unexpected "bonus," not the motive of your taking the trip in the first place—that would merely be to transfer to foreign soil the fallacies inherent in the search for the one-and-only, and to run the risk of ignoring the real opportunities for fun and adventure that travel offers.

We must recognize, though, that for some singles, meeting people of the opposite sex is a very strong motive for traveling alone. If you are one of these and you do decide that this is really why you are taking a trip, well and good, but do yourself a favor by "psyching" yourself into a realistic, balanced attitude before you start. Even though you are taking your trip to meet other singles, be aware that you will probably be getting other things from your trip, too—making friends, seeing unusual places, enjoying new experiences, etc. This is the only way of ensuring that even if you do *not* meet another single who lives up to your specifications, you will still be happy with yourself, and with your vacation.

Margot, a twenty-four-year-old New York career girl, took her first trip alone—to Bermuda—more as an experiment in seeing how she would react than anything else. In the course of it, she quickly discovered how the pressure of feeling that you have to meet other singles can get in the way of your real enjoyment of a trip.

She was more than a little nervous at first about some of the things she had never done before—the handling of foreign exchange, getting through customs, eating in strange places with no one to talk to. She managed all right, however, until she had to go down to the dining room on the first night. Then she started to worry about being the only woman in the hotel without an escort. By the time she got to the dining room she was already regretting her position. She felt uncomfortable throughout dinner, but afterward, as she sat reading in a public room, a young man came over and introduced himself. He wasn't particularly her type, but he was pleasant enough and she was desperate for a companion.

After a few days of his company, however, she realized with a shock that she really wasn't having a good time with him at all; she was doing just the things her new acquaintance wanted to do so that she could have a companion. Her precious vacation time was slipping away and she hadn't even bicycled or explored the island—two of the things she wanted to do. Then, as resolute as she had been panicky, she did something she never dreamed she could do. She suddenly packed, told the desk clerk she was moving, and went to a little villa farther out on the island.

By the end of the next week she discovered she had an entirely different feeling about herself. She had done some things she wanted to do on her own and found it wasn't hard after all. She had made some new friends that she liked, and her overall self-esteem had increased as a result of taking charge of her own life.

Luckily, if you have never traveled alone before, you don't have to take on the whole project singlehandedly. First, read everything you can get your hands on that has been written about the places you're going to visit. It will enhance your enjoyment of the trip. If you are going abroad, you can also get advice and information from the consulates and travel bureaus that many countries have in the United States. They will provide similar services for you in their own countries, once you get there.

The services of a good travel agent are of great value. It comes as a surprise to many people to learn that travel agents' services are without cost. Agents make their commissions from hotels, airlines, and other carriers. So make the most of it. They will arrange travel tickets, hotel reservations, and cue you in on climate, what to wear, how to pack— everything you need to know.

BONUSES OF TRAVELING ALONE

Clearly, the advantages of traveling alone are essentially the same as those already mentioned for going out alone anywhere: You can go when and where you want to; you are free to meet people; you can let adventures happen to you; you can go somewhere on à moment's notice. In addition, there are other bonuses in traveling alone:

Choosing Not to Be with People
This is the lesson Margot learned the hard way. For more seasoned single travelers, it is often the whole point of their traveling alone—they enjoy not having to socialize when they don't want to. And this happens to be a luxury that is hard to indulge in on singles cruises or at resorts where pressure-to-pair is the main orientation.

Choosing to Be with People
The fact that you started out alone doesn't mean that you have to spend all your time by yourself. If you really do find that you crave human companionship, join a local tour for a day or two.

A single traveler almost always attracts people, and this is why so many singles wouldn't dream of traveling any other way—once they have tried it. It is an open door to friendly human contact and adventures. Don't only seek out other singles. You will find that couples, sometimes a bit bored with one another after a couple of weeks of the kind of constant closeness which they don't have at home, are eager to have a new person to tell their adventures to.

Letting Your Hair Down
If you are traveling alone, feeling relaxed and good about the world and yourself, you are more likely to be at ease than you might among the folks back home. A man or a woman might flirt a little, offer a drink or a compliment to a stranger

or someone he has just met, and feel reasonably sure that there is no danger of embarrassment if he or she experiments a bit with a slightly different pattern of behavior.

HINTS FOR MEETING PEOPLE

Naturally even travelers who value their privacy like to be with compatible people some of the time. The art of traveling happily is to be with people when you wish and *not* to be with people when it doesn't suit you. For those occasions when you do desire companionship, here are some ideas that have helped other singles find like-minded people wherever in the world they happen to be.

Follow Your Own Interests

The very best way, as always, is to do the things you genuinely enjoy doing. Thus, a Sierra Club hiking trip or a junket down the Colorado River if you are a nature buff, a bird-watching cruise to the Caribbean if you are an amateur ornithologist, or a gourmet tour of French restaurants if you especially like to cook or eat—whatever your tastes, there is a trip or an activity that will put you in contact with others who share them.

One never-married young man of twenty-six devised an ingenious plan for ensuring that he would never want for friends or companions on a solo trip around the world. A tennis enthusiast, he discovered that any time he had the slightest desire for companions he had to do no more than find the nearest public tennis court. Just turning up in tennis togs with racquet usually was enough to ensure both a conversation and a game. And very often his new-found friends, wanting to introduce him to their way of life, would invite him home to tea or dinner. He found that the local chess club was another place he could go where he could be with people and enjoy himself.

Get Letters of Introduction

Ask friends, business acquaintances, professional colleagues, friends of friends—anyone. You never know where good leads will come from. Actively spread the word that you're taking a trip and that you would like to meet people on your way. It's amazing how many people know someone in Timbuktu, to say nothing of London and Rome.

Use the Consulates

Most foreign consulates have an officer who will be happy to assist you in meeting people you want to meet, especially if it sounds as though you plan to do some business in their country.

Contact the Concierge

Most foreign hotels have a concierge who is in charge of welcoming guests and arranging special services for them. When you arrive, seek him out and ask about special trips which he might recommend. He will probably know which of the other guests in the hotel are going where, when, and how. If you discover that someone has rented a car for the day to go to some out-of-the-way area, drop a note in his mail box and ask if you can join him—and share the expense. You'll not only get companionship but save money as well.

Avoid Airplanes

People are generally more friendly and talkative in an environment that is conducive to talk, and for whatever reason, airplanes are not one of these places. Also, natives generally travel by the less expensive means.

And if you really want to meet the people of the country, go where they play instead of where they work. People thaw in the sun. Try villages and small towns first and the big cities later in the trip.

Use Your Travel Agent

At the outset, tell your agent you are traveling alone and ask where you are most likely to encounter other interesting people—which hotels, which areas, which islands. A good agent will know these things. He will also know which resort hotels have get-acquainted parties and activities. On the other hand, if you hate planned activities and prefer a hotel where you can meet primarily the people of the country, rather than other tourists, or if you want to go to hotels frequented by other foreigners rather than Americans, be sure to let your travel agent know.

Try Singles Cruises or Resorts

As we said earlier, traveling alone for the purpose of meeting other singles is perfectly okay provided you keep it in perspective and do not let it dominate your plans or interfere with your enjoyment of places, experiences, or other people you may meet.

If you take a cruise—and they can provide a lot of fun and relaxation even with all that organized activity—try a weekend one first to see if you like it. And you may want to investigate Club Mediteranee, an organization that schedules tours and runs a chain of resorts around the world. It does not cater exclusively to singles but it has a good reputation and has become a favorite of many singles.

As for resort hotels, there are not many exclusively for

singles—yet. Many resorts are now scheduling "singles week-ends," so you might try one of these.

Of course, whether you are single or married, alone or on a tour, no matter how great your trip is, you will have your share of annoyances and inconveniences. Like life itself, a trip doesn't offer you the good times without a few of the bad. Almost everyone has to hassle with luggage these days, and travel plans sometimes go awry for everyone. Married people have each other to complain to or get mad at, as well as share the fun with, while you, as a single, may have to wait a little longer to share your experience and feelings with someone you like—either on the trip or when you get home.

We would therefore be less than candid if we did not warn you right now that there will also be times when you may feel lonely. We are, after all, human, and any human being, whether married or single, can get lonely. Usually, travelers are so busy seeing and doing things they haven't got time to be lonely—but it may hit you if you are especially fatigued, have unplanned time, or have been away from home for a long period.

Still, there are things you can do about it. We have already discussed some of these in the last chapter. If it's just a case of wanting to talk to someone, you might try what one seasoned single traveler always does—he goes down and sits in the lobby of his hotel and watches the people. He says someone invariably comes along and strikes up a conversation. If he happens to be looking at a map or guidebook, he has noticed that people are especially inclined to stop and offer their help.

Summing up, the big advantage in going out alone, and traveling alone if you choose to do so, is the opportunity it affords you for freedom and personal growth. You are fully responsible for yourself, and rather than being a handicap (as many singles consider it), this responsibility turns out to be your most valuable asset. Each time you progress in the risk taking inherent in being out on your own, you give yourself a chance to become more confident, poised, and resourceful. Each time you stick your neck out a bit instead of giving in to fear, you like yourself better. It isn't necessary to wait around for ideal circumstances, because there aren't any. A Chinese proverb says: "He who deliberates fully before taking a step will spend his entire life on one leg."

Once you have gone beyond your fears, going anywhere alone will no longer pose an overwhelming problem. You will make the decision to go or not to go solely on the basis of *your* purpose, motive, desire, and intent for your life. You will not be tyrannized in either direction. You will neither have to go out compulsively—feeling you are missing something if you don't—nor worry about yourself should you choose to stay home doing whatever interests you for several evenings or several weekends in a row. In other words, you will have become your own person, and you will make the rules for yourself. And that is how it should be.

6. Reaching Out for New Friends

Of all the ingredients that make up a successful single life, good friends must be near the top of the list. While it may be obvious why singles need friends more than married couples do, it is perhaps not so obvious that this need is actually a badge of the single's independence, and another of the apparent liabilities that can be turned into a tremendous asset, once you know how.

In marriage, husbands and wives are supposed to have each other to share good times, to bolster depressed spirits, to provide companionship and to help work out dozens of daily decisions. In addition to all the other demands and expectations we put on marriage, spouses are expected to act as each other's best friend—even as therapist in some instances.

While there is no question that in a really good marriage the two people do fulfill these roles for each other, it is by no means the rule. In fact, because of the very nature of the stresses and strains inherent in marriage, one's spouse is often the least likely person to be one's best friend. For one thing, just by virtue of the fact that the two live together, any objectivity in the way they see each other may be lost. It also frequently happens that constant proximity makes the inevitable differences in interests, temperament, and point of view stand out in painful relief. A husband may feel, for example, that his wife's time should be essentially at his disposal, while she may feel just as strongly that she should be free to make her own decisions. Is she going to ask his advice or opinion on visiting a friend or taking a course if she knows he disapproves? Probably not.

Often there just isn't enough time for spouses to be good friends to one another as domestic pressures increase and families grow. The routinized schedules and the day-to-day handling of domestic affairs into which families so easily fall may simply chip away at the reservoir of time and good will that it takes to maintain a friendship.

For the single, however, there is no ready-made confidant always on the scene. He has to pick as friends people who really meet his needs—needs which may change dramatically at various points in his life. Since a single can't fall back on the married relationship, he must learn to make the right friends and be the right kind of friend in order to satisfy the various emotional hungers which all human beings share.

Singles generally are able to rely far more on their judgment, desires, and initiative in making friends than are marrieds. Singles are also more likely to work harder at friendships, and their friends are more likely to reflect their own values and choices, since they don't have to compromise with someone else in these decisions.

FRIENDSHIPS OF MARRIED PEOPLE

Marriage is a kind of friendship, but one in which couples have a number of heavy restrictions placed on their friendships outside of marriage. At the most basic level, they have less time for friendships because much of their time is already committed to their partners. They also have less freedom to choose friends independently and spontaneously. There is always concern as to how the spouse will feel about the friend, whether the friend will fit in with the couple's lifestyle, and even whether a really close friend and the confidences shared with him are a sign of disloyalty to one's spouse.

In some marriages, outside friends are not even important. Most couples have only a few close friends, and these relationships are frequently based on associations with the parents of their children's playmates. These relationships often are confined to superficial socializing with other married couples; significant personal conversations are avoided since the complexity of always being in couples seems to preclude the sharing of much expression of feelings. As most married couples will readily admit, the relationships become too routinized.

Another typical kind of relationship starts when either the wife or the husband becomes a friend independently of his spouse. Then the spouses are brought in, and an attempt is made to cement the friendship four ways. Plenty of marriage counselors report on how this system can go awry—Bob's wife Alice finds she has nothing to say to Don's wife Betty, while Don seems to have too much in common with Alice.

The most troublesome aspect of friendships among married couples is that either the husband or the wife is decisive in choosing all the couple's friends, rather than the friends coming equally from both spouses. This usually happens when one member of the couple is not a strong person in his or her own right and does not carry a full share of responsibility in the relationship.

In Wayne's case, he and his ex-wife married young, and her friends were far-out people on the fringes of the drug culture. Most of Wayne's friends had already gone through it and were bored with it. "Eventually," said Wayne, "all of our friends were the friends I brought to the marriage. Some of her friends turned out to be extremely unstable and gradually dropped away. Others she gave up herself—I never asked her to. But once she did, she resented me for having to do it. I resented her for the kinds of friends she had and for not being an equal partner in our relationship."

Sometimes a husband may be totally immersed in his work and welcome the fact that his wife does all the social planning for them both. Even if he's unhappy with her choices, he may tolerate her friends and not bother to contribute anyone to their social pool, making the development of friendships a great burden to his wife.

More commonly, the husband makes social contacts in his work while his wife, living in cloistered housewifery, does not, and there outside friendships become mainly a matter of serving his business needs. The result can be that he develops a social life and a group of friends that are mainly his own and his wife begins to feel extraneous and socially inept. Whichever member of the married pair dominates a relationship, the imbalance itself is likely to lead to stresses, strains, and finally resentments on the part of both people.

Of course, some marriages allow for such freedom and do not have these problems. Both partners may just naturally like and attract the same kind of people, and multiple, meaningful friendships can develop. Such couples would seem to have the best of both possible worlds, and there is no question that a marriage of this kind can be a wonderful thing. Realistically, however, most marriages are not that wonderful, and the quality of the friendships most couples have is not that good.

FRIENDS—THE SINGLE'S FAMILY

It is possible to live without friends, of course, and people have done it or have had to do it from time to time, but most everyone agrees it is certainly not very pleasant. Once we discover the pleasures of friendship—and this doesn't always happen in our early years—it surely emerges as one of the great joys of our lives.

For some, however, friendship may be more work than for others. For example, a never-married in his or her twenties may make friends more easily and have more friends available than a recently divorced woman of forty or a widow of fifty-three. This is hardly surprising—after all, the never-married has been single for a lifetime and has had much experience making friends. The divorced and widowed, however, have only just emerged from marriage and have to make a new beginning in an unfamiliar single world. But that need only be a temporary situation. The ability to make friends— friends that *you* desire and want (as contrasted with those that may not interest you especially but who seek you out)—can be developed.

There is no magic formula for friendship. What it comes down to is being thoughtful, being there when you're needed, and taking the initiative in getting outside of yourself and thinking of the other person even when it may not be convenient. But you only become aware of such things when you are aware of your own need for friends, and singles, just because they are single, are obliged to confront and directly deal with this need.

The most successful single people in "Challenge" workshops are usually those who share confidences, ideas, experiences, and feelings with one or more friends. They also regard these friends with the kind of profound affection and closeness one usually associates with a warm, close-knit family. They sometimes do a better job of taking care of one another than real families do.

Indeed, friends are the single's family. We are speaking here of a new kind of family, one that is not built around kinship or marriage relationships but around real preference, shared interests, and genuine affection. This kind of family in its most extreme form is reflected in the commune movement, which is actually less of a back-to-the-land movement than an attempt to find familial closeness with those we respond to and those who respond to us.

With or without a commune, a family of friends that gives one a special sense of belonging is accessible to everyone, but especially to singles. Even if you are essentially a loner, you will probably want a few people around occasionally. How you go about making friends will be taken up in later sections of this chapter, but first we want to throw some new light on a question you may not have asked yourself.

WHY DO WE NEED FRIENDS?

Friendships mean different things to us at different times in our lives. When we are very young, we take friends for granted: they are there to amuse us, have fun with, share secrets and confidences with, and "collect" as we might charms for a bracelet—as a badge of popularity, a living proof of our self-worth. But as we mature, we come to appreciate what friends mean and the roles they play in our lives.

Companionship is usually the aspect of friendship that most singles put at the top of their list. Good companions allow us to be ourselves at the same time that we enjoy their company. They don't overwhelm us with either their presence or their needs. They are fun to be with, and they make doing something we enjoy more enjoyable. And they are there because they like us and care about us.

In times of crisis or stress, support is what we want from friends. Just to know that someone understands and cares is often enough to see us through all kinds of troubles. In difficult moments, friends can help supply that crucial bit of life affirmation that makes all the difference.

It is not just to help us through our troubles that we need friends. We all yearn for people with whom we can rejoice in our successes, in whose eyes and words we see our triumphs recorded and even magnified.

Friends keep our minds alive and help us to expand our ideas and explore other ways of looking at our world. They are a source of change and growth; in sharing their lives, we become more than we could be on our own.

While we may easily overestimate the extent to which interests and activities need to be shared in order to be enjoyed, there is no question that comparing notes on outlooks, interests, experiences, or ideas can be a great pleasure. We have all had animated conversations that ensue when we run across a kindred spirit—someone who has a similar taste for and knowledge about one of our pet topics. It is like meeting a fellow countryman in a foreign land. Such people are worth seeking out, and certainly worth holding onto as friends, once they are found.

Finally, good friends help us to define ourselves and ultimately to accept ourselves. This self-definition process through others starts almost from the moment of birth. Certainly from the first moment that we notice there is someone else in the sandbox, we start to perceive and define ourselves in terms of our interaction with other people, both inside and outside the family. In experiments with children, it has been found that beyond a certain age the relationships a child has with its peer group and friends become more significant than those it has with its parents.

If you allow someone to understand you, all the endless role playing and routinized remarks and behavior can be left behind. You can permit yourself to appear as you really are to someone else, and this is one of the most effective and pleasurable ways known of accepting and affirming yourself. By providing, accepting, clarifying, reflecting, and occasionally correcting our "real" feelings and thoughts, particularly those we are still struggling with, friends help us see and understand ourselves.

DIFFERENT FRIENDS FOR DIFFERENT THINGS

No one should expect to get all these needs filled by just one person. On the other hand, we don't need to have a large number of friends at any one time to feel our lives enriched. Even three or four really good friends are all most people usually make in a lifetime. Good friendships take time to develop and time to maintain, but this should not keep us from realizing the advantages of enjoying as many friendships as we can with a number of different people.

As you become more successfully single, you will become better at attracting as wide a variety of friends as the needs of your personality require, and each one of these can share one or more of your interests. These can be married, single, separated, same sex, opposite sex, student, businessman, professional, artist, and, ideally, of varying ages and races. This obviously does not mean you will see all of them all the time, even if you could. But even when you do not keep in constant touch, just knowing they are there, ready when you need them, as you are ready for them, is a part of their meaning to you.

Some friends will be great to talk to about everyday affairs; some will be for socializing and fun; some for ruminating about the state of life, love, and eternity over a glass of wine; some for joking and laughing with; some for seeing movies and plays with; and some—the very best and the special few—for those occasions when you feel more than a little low and need someone who really understands.

Not all friends can be "good" for everything, just as no man or woman can be the perfect spouse, fulfilling all the needs of the other. If we like someone, it is foolish to be disappointed if he or she can't fulfill all our desires or needs. It is the better part of wisdom to appreciate one's friends for those qualities you like and value and for whatever they can contribute to your life within their limitations of time and personality.

You will probably have a spectrum of friends, some of whom will be more important to you than others, but all of whom you will genuinely care about. If all your friends were "best friends," it would require an emotional intensity you might have difficulty sustaining and fitting into your everyday life of commitments and obligations.

It is wise to be careful of the temptations of trying to turn a close friend into the one-and-only friend. It is easy to be tempted because if you like someone very much you naturally gravitate toward him or her, but then your friend's slightest failing can be blown way out of proportion in relation to his or her good qualities. If you have other friends that you see, you won't put such a burden on your special friend. You can allow him the same "space" and freedom you need from him. It may require a little more time and risk taking to cultivate more than one good friend, but in the long run you will be protecting all your friendships and enjoying all of them more. If you let yourself get lazy in this respect, however, you may be doing no more than transferring the search for the one-and-only "other" into the search for the one-and-only friend.

ABANDONING THE SEARCH FOR THE ONE-AND-ONLY

One of the great obstacles to having friends if you are single is the ill-advised search for the one-and-only "other" of the opposite sex. When we are searching for one "great relationship" that will supposedly solve all our problems, other relationships hardly seem to matter except as they may contribute to that search. The idea of the one-and-only *anything* always invests situations or persons with more than they can reasonably be expected to deliver. The more friends you have and the more people you know, the more likely you are to perceive others clearly and not invest anyone— because of your own inner needs—with qualities, attributes, or talents that are simply not there in actuality.

Going steady as a teen-ager or rushing into an exclusive relationship too soon after divorce or widowhood usually means you are grabbing at the security of a known quality—a comfortable relationship—and denying yourself the new experiences with a number of people which are necessary if you are to garner the knowledge and insight you need about yourself and others.

The search for the one-and-only always preempts the possibility of the unexpected. A single young attorney we know went to a political fund-raising rally, as he went everywhere, with the idea of finding the one-and-only uppermost in his mind. After surveying the assemblage and not seeing any woman who visually matched his image of the perfect mate, he announced to a friend, "There's no girl here for me," and left. He wasn't fair to himself. There might have been a woman there whom he would have liked knowing, even though she wasn't his ideal, plus a couple of men who might have turned into good friends, plus a few fellow lawyers who might have been interesting for him to know, *plus* he might have had a good time.

One trouble with such a search is that it is usually based on preconceptions of who our potential mate is and even what he or she will look like. But when singles get together in workshops or just in the course of life itself, they find these stereotypes don't hold up. The never-married who feel they have nothing in common with the divorced or widowed, begin to see them as "people," as individuals, apart from their labels. In a similar manner, age differences break down and singles find that there can be great rewards when a wise, experienced fifty-year-old becomes friends with an exuberant, idealistic twenty-three-year-old. Sometimes, the people who impress us least in a hurried meeting turn out to be the most impressive later, and vice-versa. Allow yourself to come into contact with the unexpected, for you will be opening the door to new friendships.

DO YOU KNOW WHO YOUR FRIENDS ARE?

At this point in your life, you may have many friends or a few. The quantity isn't important but the quality is. Are you holding on to some of your friends and continuing to see them even though you no longer particularly like being with them? It sometimes happens that we grow apart from people we once liked a great deal, but out of misguided loyalty, lethargy, or perhaps even nostalgia, we maintain the friendship long after the reason for its existence has passed.

Perhaps it never occurred to you to sit down and analyze who your friends are and, in each case, what they mean to you. Such an idea may even seem crass, yet some singles in the workshops have found it opened their eyes for the first time to who their friends really were and to the possibility of friendship with others whom it had never occurred to them to cultivate as friends. We can assure you that this exercise, honestly carried out, may be of considerable value.

Take a sheet of blank paper and draw a line down the middle. On one side, put a heading: "People who make me feel good (happy, uplifted, positive)." On the other side, put: "People who make me feel bad (unhappy, irritable, negative) or neutral."

Before putting down any names on either side, think about each person for a few minutes and remember those recent times you have been together or talked on the telephone. Concentrate, too, on how you would feel about the idea of being with that particular person again. What feelings come to mind? Are they those of pleasure and enjoyment? Or do you sense (perhaps to your dismay) a vague uneasiness or even annoyance?

Take time to tune in to your feelings about each person. Is your relationship equal—are you both giving and getting from each other? Do you really look forward to seeing your friend or are you just following an established social pattern? If you didn't see the person again, would it matter to you? Can you count on this individual if you need companionship or advice, and are you ready to be there when he or she needs you, not out of duty, not in payment for friendship, but because you want to? If more of the feelings you experience are positive than negative (or vice-versa), you will have no trouble in placing him or her in the proper column.

You may be asking, "Why should I bother with such a procedure in the first place?" It is because we all have so little time for the truly important things in our lives that we should want to spend it in the most profitable and enjoyable way possible. Friends who "bring us down" or dissipate our energy, add nothing to our lives. We will be happier when free of them.

Allen, a thirty-two-year-old single, said it this way: "I had half a dozen people whom I considered pretty good friends. Four of them were 'couple' friends that my ex-wife and I used to dine with, play cards with, or go to ball games with. After my divorce, I still went out with them occasionally, but Frank, particularly would always end up an evening with joking innuendos about my being interested in his wife. I was not at all. I don't know if he was jealous of everyone, or just me, or if he was just being funny.

"Anyway, when I gave myself the test and started writing down friends' names on that Friendship Evaluation sheet, it suddenly hit me that Frank was bugging the hell out of me and I resented him. I hadn't been aware of it at all until I really began sorting out who my friends were and weren't. Instead of enjoying his company, I found I was beginning to dread being around him at all. It was several months ago that I realized all this, and since then I've stopped seeing him."

Real friends build your self-esteem and help you like yourself better. Maybe, like Allen, you've been harboring some deep resentments about some of your "friends"—friends who no longer qualify as such. Since genuine friends deserve so much of your time, anyway, why waste it on those who are not good for you?

If *you* don't make these decisions about your friendships, who will make them for you? It may seem heartless to objectively appraise relationships in this way, but you will be doing yourself and your friends a favor in the long run. And you will be saving yourself precious time because, if the friendship is basically no longer a good one, it will eventually break down of its own accord—but perhaps only after you have invested more time and energy on it than it deserves.

Don't dwell on how "sad" it is to give up old friends. Think about how great you will feel when you have new and better ones. It's the difference between a subsistence diet that just gets you by and a rich, varied cuisine that is both nourishing and stimulating.

On your Friendship Evaluation list, also put the names of the people whom you don't count as friends but just as acquaintances. Those in the positive column are ones you should seek out, in order to see if the potential that you sense for a good relationship can be developed into something more than it is at this time.

PLATONIC FRIENDS ARE POSSIBLE

The failure to develop platonic friendships is a major flaw in the modus operandi of many singles, both men and women. Platonic love and, by extension, platonic friendship, is defined in *Encyclopaedia Britannica* as "an affectionate relationship between a man and a woman into which the sexual element does not enter."

Most singles have at least a few friends with whom to share their joys, accomplishments, misgivings, and disappointments, but these friends are usually of the same sex. One of the more pleasant discoveries you will make as you come into your own as a single person is that, contrary to popular mythology, platonic friendships are indeed possible. Once you learn how to develop them, you will wonder how you managed without them.

One single woman complained, "I have more female friends than I know what to do with but practically no male friends." Similarly, single men often accumulate a lot of male friends to share their business or recreational interests. But very few singles of either sex have nearly enough platonic friends—if, indeed, they have one.

If you have never thought about having platonic friends because you thought such friendships couldn't exist, begin by trying to change your perspective of the man-woman relationship. Singles are in a much better position to do this than most married people because they have much more of the emotional freedom needed to analyze their relationships with the opposite sex. They are more likely to be free of any vested interest in the traditional state of marriage and the point of view that goes with it.

Of course, it is our marriage-minded society that created and continues to support the myth that men and women cannot be close friends without the factor of sex entering in. The myth is obviously useful in restricting people to one-man—one-woman relationships by making any opposite-sex friendship outside marriage so subject to suspicion that it is often not worth the trouble. The almost universal acceptance of this myth has unfortunately brought many singles to believe that platonic friendships are impossible, too, with the result that they may never have exercised the emotional freedom mentioned above.

At one "Challenge" meeting a divorcée of thirty-five was confronted by a slightly younger divorced engineer named Bob, who had expressed his utter astonishment at the idea: "What! Platonic friends! There is no such animal. There's always a sexual element. If not immediately, then very soon afterward. That's the way we're made!"

The divorcée replied, "Nonsense! There are a lot of men I have absolutely no sexual interest in whatsoever. Jack is one. He has a sailboat. I don't have one. I like sailing, I'm a good sailor and he knows it—I'm better than some of his male buddies. If I happen to be free on a weekend and his usual male friends are not available, or even when they are, he may call me. If I'm free, I go. He has no more sexual interest in me than I have in him and we both know it, but we *like* each other. You don't have to want to go to bed with every man you know just because he's male and you're female. If the chemistry isn't there, it isn't there. And when it's not, you both know it."

The engineer shot back, "That's all very well for you to say. You're a woman, and platonic friendships are probably easier for women. But I can assure you no red-blooded male is going to tolerate a situation like that for long."

A widowed man in his early forties spoke up: "Oh, I don't know. I think I'm pretty red-blooded and I not only can tolerate such relationships, I like them. When I was married, my wife and I worked different hours, and there were several women I worked with, single as well as married, that I got to be pretty good friends with. Sometimes we had dinner, once we went bowling, and a couple of times we all went to the movies together. Of course, it was a group, and that may have made a difference.

"But since I've been a widower, I've developed a number of platonic friendships with individual women who share my interests. It isn't always easy. Sometimes, you've got to set up ground rules. For example, if I'm really attracted to a woman sexually, I have to know where I stand, sooner or later. Once the air is cleared, we can go on from there."

It seems that we are left to discover on our own that platonic friendships are possible, not only by taking a personal stand against the prevailing myths, but also by making a real effort to understand how and why we can be friends with a particular person of the opposite sex without lapsing automatically into various forms of sex role behavior.

What Blocks Platonic Friendships?

It is hardly surprising that most singles don't have enough platonic friends—after all, it is only now that we are at a point historically and culturally where such friendships seem to be truly possible. Only recently have we shaken loose from centuries-old prejudice, sexism, and rigid role playing— wherein women are seen as inferior and treated as sex objects, and men are seen as predators and treated with suspicion—to arrive at the point where we may enjoy each other as people, irrespective of whether we are male or female. That, in a larger sense, is what platonic friendship is all about.

Since most of us are still so new at it, if indeed we believe it is possible at all, we approach it gingerly. While it is the most natural thing in the world to have platonic friendships, we are so brain-washed by the idea of automatic and invariable sexual pairing under any and all circumstances that we usually can't see this readily.

Another set of obstacles standing in the way of making platonic friendships involves our ego expectations, especially those traditionally linked to sex—those strong feelings usually associated with our idea of our own attractiveness as a sexual partner. For instance, a man may think making a pass is expected of him, that his image as a male is at stake, that he will be hurting the woman's feelings if he doesn't, or even that she may think he is a homosexual. However, the simple truth may be that he likes her as a friend but is not interested in sexual involvement, for whatever reason.

A woman, on the other hand, often feels that if she doesn't show some sexual interest in a man, he will conclude that she's frigid or doesn't like him and will stop calling her. If he shows no interest in her, she may fear it is because she's too unattractive, too old, too young, too independent—any number of doubts having to do with her femininity and desirability.

The possibilities for both sexes are endless, and so is the confusion, until you get what's happening straight in your own mind and, if necessary, discuss it with your friends.

Of course, the most obvious obstacle to forming a platonic friendship is a strong sexual need that naturally gets directed at a friend of the opposite sex. Sex is, after all, an expression of affection, which is what we feel for our friends. However, it is not the *only* way of expressing affection. The never-marrieds have been coping with these needs all their adult lives and generally have them in some degree of balance or adjustment. It is those who have recently become single—the divorced and widowed—who during marriage (unless the marriage was totally unrewarding) were generally accustomed to some degree of emotional support and sexual satisfaction. Consequently, they may especially crave the security and comfort of a close sexual relationship which would seem to solve all their needs.

The practical and psychological advantages of platonic friendships are easily worth the effort you may have to exert in order to overcome the obstacles that keep you from developing such friends. Indeed, it is a knack or art to acquire them, especially if you've never done it before—no question about it. But once you have acquired this technique, it will immeasurably extend the boundaries and enjoyment level of your single life.

Why Have Platonic Friendships?

Platonic friendships offer all the advantages of any other friendship, plus these extra bonuses:

> They enrich your intellectual and emotional life by broadening the potential base of your friendships and expanding the range and variety of the people you know.

> They allow you to ease up on sexual role playing—a significant advantage since we seem to imbibe games, guile, and sex-linked "tricks" almost with mother's milk. In being straightforward with the opposite sex, we can often explore elements of our own personalities in greater depth than if we feel we have to be "on" all the time.

> They provide you with the point of view of the opposite sex without the confusion of sexual issues. We've already talked about the validation and self-definition that occurs when we bounce our ideas and personality

off another person. Think how one-sided the picture is if there are not both men and women friends in our lives with whom we can do this!

For a man, it can mean a special sense of relief and relaxation to know that he need not be forever making a pass at a woman in order to prove his virility or to make certain that no one suggests that he is in some way odd.

For a woman, knowing she is appreciated for her own self rather than as a sex object (which pairing pressure promotes) gives her a chance to experience a new dimension of her own identity.

For both sexes, having platonic friends "defuses" the insidious search for the one-and-only, allowing them to relax together and to begin enjoying the unique benefits of being single.

Finally, platonic friends provide for special social needs. Since a lot of our society is still built around pairing, mating, and dating, and does not yet include "single-ing," both men and women will sometimes need an opposite-sex companion for a variety of social events.

Developing Platonic Friendships

There is so much variability in the way platonic friendships actually develop that there are no hard and fast rules for how you go about making them. To some extent, you just let it happen—as you do with same-sex friendships—but a positive attitude which "sees" such friendships as both possible and good for you is perhaps the greatest factor in helping them to happen.

If you have never had a platonic friend, or enough of

them, take a little time to analyze why this is so. Are you closing the door on such relationships because you are really searching for the one-and-only and thus perceiving the other person as a potential lover whether or not he may, in fact, be one or develop into one? Are your emotional needs so great that you regard such platonic relationships as "inferior" to love affairs and therefore not worth the trouble? If you do have a platonic relationship, are you burdening it with some of the old sexist role-playing games; that is, does it bother you if you must pay half the check or if your friend is unavailable when you call or need him or her?

If for any reason there is tension between you and an opposite-sex acquaintance who might become a platonic friend—if you think he or she is interested in a sex relation-ship but you are not—by all means, talk it out! It's not as embarrassing as you may think. Clearing the air gives you confidence and a feeling of self-liking as you become profi-cient at it.

A divorcée in a "Challenge" workshop explained that honesty is always necessary in forming platonic relationships. When she is very fond of a man who does not appeal to her sexually, she simply tells him directly, "I think you're a wonderful man and an attractive man and I value our friend-ship a great deal, but I don't really want our relationship to take on all the complexities of our becoming lovers. Still, if we can be friends, I would very much like us to be." She says a few men never call her back, but a surprising number do, and they have become good friends. A few have even said that they felt an enormous sense of relief in not having to "perform" automatically as the sexual aggressor.

A never-married man told of his experience with platonic friendships: "I had a longtime on-going intimate relationship with a girl I cared a lot about, but it ended when she had a chance to take an unusual two-year job overseas. It was something she wanted very badly. Since that time I've met a girl in my apartment complex whom I really enjoy being with. We play tennis almost every weekend but I'm not sexually interested in her at all.

"She indicated early in the relationship that she *was* interested, and when this happened, there was just no way out but to sit down and talk to her about it. It wasn't easy. The most important thing is to be careful about hurting the other person's feelings. I told her I wasn't ready yet to start a new intimate relationship, and I pointed out to her that she should be pleased that my interest in her wasn't as a sex object. I talked about the advantages in a nonsexual relationship and finally asked her to please remain my friend. She did, and there was no strain or embarrassment about it whatsoever once the air was cleared.

"Then I heard from my old girl friend that she suddenly decided not to come back to the States at all. And I discovered, about the same time, that I was developing a strong attraction for my tennis-playing friend. I used to think if the 'spark' wasn't there immediately, it was no-go, but I was wrong. Our platonic friendship has actually blossomed into a close intimate relationship."

Sometimes the sequence is just the opposite. Jeanne, a department store salesgirl, was separated from her husband when she started dating Keith, her department manager, a divorced man. They were strongly attracted to each other and almost immediately began an affair. It lasted almost a year, until he began pressuring her to get married. When she realized she didn't want to get married, the affair soon dwindled down, especially since Keith seemed to have a real need to get married.

Their sexual relationship ceased, but they continued to see

each other as friends as they gradually came to realize that they still liked each other a lot and had a great deal in common. He never did marry, but they have continued as friends for four years now, helping each other out in times of trouble and, in general, sharing the camaraderie and good feeling that friends generally share with each other.

"Some of my girl friends think this is hard to do," says Jeanne. "They think once you've had an affair with someone, anything else is a let-down. With me, it seems the most natural thing in the world to remain friends with an ex-lover if the man really liked you in the beginning. After all, if you like each other well enough to have a sexual relationship, you ought to like each other well enough to be good friends when it's over. I don't believe in 'burning bridges' behind me. To me, at any rate, the people I like are special—no matter what happened between us."

Being platonic friends, after all, need not mean that you feel no sexual attraction at all for that person. The attraction may indeed exist, but for a variety of reasons you may both decide to do nothing about it. For one thing, you may work together (usually an awkward situation), or one of you could be married, or there could be other commitments that preclude it. A relationship such as this may be harder to maintain, but it could prove equally rewarding to you both.

Sarah, a forty-year-old divorcée who works as a computer programmer for a large company, feels she "lost out" on a valuable relationship with a former boss simply because she didn't know how to cope with a platonic relationship or—more to the point—her own feelings. Hers might be an example of what not to do.

"It could never happen now," says Sarah. "I've learned too much in the last few years. But then I was just divorced, and so anxious to succeed in a high-powered job, I guess I thought I had to appear totally businesslike to do it. Anyway, Brian is the manager who hired me. We liked each other right away—and we had extraordinary rapport and so many interests in common. The problem was what to do about it. None of this was ever openly expressed, you understand.

"He was married and I was so intent on never showing any personal interest I behaved like a robot. If I could ever have relaxed or if we even could have talked about it a little during one of the few times it seemed to come up naturally, it probably would have relieved the pressure between us and we might still have been friends. Once at lunch the subject almost came up, but I changed the topic abruptly to cover my embarrassment. Finally, so much tension built up and we behaved so artificially around each other, the situation became impossible. We became more like enemies than friends. Finally, he moved up in the corporation and out of my department.

"The funny part about all this is that an associate of mine—a rather open, direct woman who really wasn't anywhere as close to him as I was—has remained friendly with him, even today. The difference? She was confident, natural, and unafraid of being 'misinterpreted.' She told me later she once forthrightly discussed with him the realistic problems of two people attracted to one another, working together but not open to a sexual liaison.

"I now think that people—women especially—shouldn't try to appear like bloodless paragons in the office or executive suite. Not that being flirtatious or always on the make is the answer—I don't think anyone could keep people's respect that way. On the other hand, I don't think you should try to curb all your natural feelings, either. There is a way to live with them comfortably, and I suspect now it has lots to do with expressing them verbally from time to time rather than holding them in."

Once you have come to terms with your sexual feelings

and trust yourself to respond with ease, naturalness, and sense of appropriateness, which is a large part of the knack of handling platonic friendships with singles and marrieds, you may well find yourself better able to handle same-sex friendships as well.

People of both sexes often want to be friends with one another even more than they want to be lovers, parent-surrogates, the one-and-only, or anything else. Singles who manage their single lives most successfully have a lot of platonic friends because they have learned how much such friends contribute to their lives.

THE ART OF DEALING WITH MARRIED FRIENDS

One of the most common complaints that singles make is that they have difficulty maintaining friendships with married couples. This is especially true for the newly divorced and widowed who are not yet psychologically out of the married world although they are physically part of the singles community. As their friendships from the married years begin to deteriorate, as they generally do, they feel the loss of contact and a sense that they must be less desirable than they used to be or their friends wouldn't be dropping them from their circle.

There are many reasons why it is difficult for singles to maintain close friendship with married couples. We have already mentioned how singles frequently want more from friendships than individuals in a marriage can readily give. Singles are also seen as a threat to marriage for other reasons. Having someone around who is single, full of life, and "growing" can be just too threatening for couples having marital discord; they may fear that the attractions of the single life will contribute to the breaking up of the marriage.

A wife may be jealous of a male single friend of her husband who takes so much of her husband's time in business or recreation that she feels not enough time is left over for her. A husband may feel that his wife is devoting "his time" to her friends. Sexual rivalry is an important inhibitor of such friendships, too. The married woman's reasoning goes like this: All single women really want to get married; therefore keep an eye on your husband if any are around or, better still, make sure there never are any single women around. For the married man, the "logic" is comparable : All single men are basically sexual predators; therefore leave your wife alone with a single man only at the peril of your marriage. This thinking, of course, is far too stereotyped to be accurate. But because it is common, it should be recognized that it arises from, and is perpetuated by, a pressure-to-pair society which colors almost all relationships with sexual hues.

Hal, a thirty-three-year-old never-married, described his experience this way: "Bob and I were classmates and we've been good friends for fifteen years. I don't even care much for his new wife, and I certainly have no sexual interest in her. Lately, though, whenever they invite me to dinner, Hal seems piqued if I even talk to her. If I say anything complimentary to her, he really gets upset and jokingly accuses me of being after his wife. But it's no joke to him."

It is often a test of just how mature or healthy a marriage is to see how husband and wife handle a single friend, male or female—particularly a friend who has just become single. If the marriage is open and honest, with the two partners feeling good about themselves and each other, a single friend can be a marvelous experience, cueing them into other worlds and activities different from their own. If the marriage is shaky and one or both of the partners is insecure, any single may be seen as a danger or threat. So don't be surprised if some of these friendships do not survive, no matter what you do. After all, friendships are based on many forms of sharing, and just as singles have a community that should naturally bring them closer together, so married couples are apt to find their closest friends among other married couples who share their common concern and interests.

How can you, as a single, enhance your relationship with married couples? One thing you can do is try to see their point of view in dealing with you as a single person. Because they generally think in terms of pairs, they may automatically assume that they must find a date for you if they are giving a dinner party—or they ask you to "bring someone."

When this happens to singles, some resent not being accepted as a person in their own right. It may not have occurred to your married friends that you want to come alone, and the simplest way to resolve this is just to tell them what your feelings are. They will very likely have no objections if they are good friends.

Mark, a thirty-five-year-old never-married, was invited to a dinner party by his married friends, who added as an automatic afterthought, "Oh . . . and bring a date." As a single, Mark had naturally heard this many times before. But this time he was aware of a rising anger, perhaps because he had just broken up with a long-time girlfriend and had no ready date available. The next day, since it was still on his mind, he decided to call his friends up and tell them how he felt.

The conversation went something like this:

MARK: Hello Bill, is Martha there? Could you get her on the other phone? I need to talk to both of you about something that is bothering me.

BILL: Okay. . . . Martha. . . . Here she is—what is it?

MARK: Well, I don't know just how to say this. It's a little thing, really, but it's been bugging me, and I thought maybe we should talk it out. It's about my bringing a date to your party next Saturday night. I know that's usually expected of a single man, but . . . well . . . I wonder why it should be? Right now, there's no one I can think of that I want to bring—and anyway isn't this a bit of a cliché? Shouldn't a single person be enough in his own right? Why does there have to be "two" of me?

BILL: Why—I don't know. I never thought about it.

MARTHA: I just assumed you wanted to come with somebody.

MARK: I'd rather come alone than invite someone I don't care that much about—just to be part of a couple.

MARTHA: It never occurred to us that you would feel that way. But now that you mention it, it seems logical that it would be annoying to always be asked to "bring somebody."

MARK: Right. It is. But even I never realized it till now.

MARTHA: Good. I'm glad you brought the subject up. We really don't need an extra person. I guess we just automatically think in terms of couples. But I can see it doesn't have to be this way. It's you we want.

Besides leveling with your married friends so that they realize that you are indeed a person in your own right, there are other things you can do for them to enhance your relationship—little kindnesses that are not mere reciprocity but that indicate a real desire to expand the intimacy of your friendship. What about offering to baby-sit with a married couple's child for a day or an evening—or if the child is a little older, offering to take him for an outing for a day or a weekend? It will give the parents some much needed time off, for which they will certainly be grateful. In fact, for some beleaguered parents, this is a more valued gift than any you might buy in a store.

The same is true of house sitting or pet sitting. When people go away on a trip, they feel so much better if there is someone to keep an eye on their place and perhaps water the plants. Since the single friend's freedom is greater, he can more easily do this.

Such kindnesses certainly should not be interpreted as "buying one's way" with married friends. It is simply something nice you can do for a friend whose other married friends are apt to have a life more crowded with domestic details than yours.

If you know you want to be married, however, be aware of a small emotional hazard in being this closely involved with married friends. The home of a happily married couple may be a somewhat painful reminder to you of what you want your life to be like ultimately. However, it can also make you aware of how much additional compromise is required when there are children. In all, it may end up making you more (rather than less) content with your single life and more determined than ever to enjoy and savor it while you can.

MAKING FRIENDS WITH CHILDREN

As some singles get older, particularly those who have never married, they often feel an acute sense of missing something important as they contemplate the fact that they are not going to have any children. In fact, they may jump into an unwise marriage for the primary purpose of having children "before it's too late." There are so many unwanted and neglected children around who would benefit from your interest that there is logically no real need to parent a child of your own in order to satisfy your desire to love and nurture a child.

If the need for a child is strong enough, you may want to adopt one. This is now possible for a single, although it still isn't easy. Short of that, if you want a real relationship with a child, there are many ways to arrange to be a part-time parent. The most obvious place to begin is with your married friends, who will probably be delighted to have you take the children off their hands for a few hours. The advantage of this is that you can enjoy all the pleasures of being with children with none of the heavy everyday responsibilities which can so burden real parents.

Gwen, a forty-year-old never-married, had a career that was going well. She had no particular desire to get married, but she realized that she was more than a little wistful about the probability of never having any children. Her solution was to "borrow" two of her friend's children for an entire weekend once a month. "When I deliver them home on Sunday night, I know they've had fun and I've been to places and done things I would never do by myself. Their parents couldn't be more grateful. I find that it's just enough 'mothering' to keep me satisfied—until the next time."

Some single men, too, find enjoyment in being a part-time parent. For example, Sam, a never-married man of thirty-two, had no desire to marry but nevertheless loved being with children. He had thought about adopting one but gave up the idea when he realized the difficulties involved. He resolved this by being a part-time parent for the twelve-year-old son of a married couple living in his apartment complex. Sam played a lot of tennis and since the young boy was eager to learn—and neither of his parents were athletic—it was a happy solution for everyone when Sam took him under his wing and taught him the game.

There are other ways of befriending children besides taking out the children of your married friends. You can join a Big Brother organization and spend time with a child who really needs you. Scout troops are actively seeking adults without children to serve as leaders. Don't overlook the possibility of volunteer work at a children's hospital. If you contact a local family service organization, dozens of opportunities to fulfill at least some of your parenting needs will present themselves.

Some singles, especially men, say they would like to do some of these things with children but they are afraid of being suspected of having ulterior motives. This type of thinking is perhaps inevitable (and probably even somewhat realistic) in our sex-role stereotyped society, and there is not a great deal you can do on your own to change it. You should not, however, let it dominate your actions and allow it to cheat you out of what might be a highly beneficial relationship for you and a child.

BEING YOUR OWN FRIEND

All of this takes us back to one of our major themes: self-acceptance. Now that you have begun to feel it is really okay to be single, you are able to like yourself more. You can now become "your own best friend," and give yourself the same kindness, tolerance, forgiveness, attentiveness, and consideration that you give your friends. The necessity for doing this may seem obvious, but it usually is overlooked.

You can be your own inspiration and have a good time wherever you are, whether or not anyone else is around. You can be your own strength, comfort, and source of encouragement. You can give yourself good counsel and advice. Nice as it is to have friends there to do things for us, we *can* do these things for ourselves. And many times, we must.

Most of us are much more critical of ourselves than anyone else. Few of us take the time to indulge in self-congratulation, even when most appropriate. Congratulating yourself may sound like a frivolous idea, but when you take the trouble to do it, you will glow, just as you might in the wake of a friend's appreciation. So pat yourself on the back when you've accomplished something difficult or when you've practiced some risk taking that was hard to do. Begin to see and appreciate yourself for what you are.

Show your appreciation for yourself by giving yourself a present from time to time. It will be particularly enjoyable on those occasions when you've reached a goal you've set for yourself or accomplished something that took a lot of courage. Don't wait for something big—sometimes a very small act or achievement deserves a reward.

Dorothy, recently divorced after twenty-two years of marriage, carried out the workshop suggestion of rewarding herself and told this story: "It may seem insignificant to other people, but it was a big event for me when I decided to have Thanksgiving dinner. I invited several single people from my office to join me. I had always been with other couples on special holidays when I was married and I didn't know any singles socially. So when four out of the five I invited said 'yes' and the dinner turned out to be a success and everybody had a good time, I decided I deserved a present. The next day I went out and bought myself a small mirror that I had just seen in an antique shop but which I considered an extravagance under normal circumstances. Every time I look in it and remember how I acquired it, I feel good."

Another "Challenge" workshop participant, a single aerospace engineer who is usually too busy to indulge a passion for science fiction, treats himself to several volumes and an uninterrrupted weekend of reading pleasure whenever he finishes a particularly difficult technical paper.

Does being your own best friend seem like a tall order? Do you wonder if you can do it? More than a few singles have learned how. Look at the advantage—when you learn to be your own best friend, you have a friend for life.

7. How Singles Meet Singles

When the subject of improving one's social life arises, the question singles most often ask is, "How should I go about meeting other singles?" For many singles, the question they are really asking is, "Where is my one-and-only?" We hope this book will help you to get beyond this so that the question will become simply, "Where are all the people I can have as friends?"

It is a natural enough question. Of course, singles want to meet other singles. Theoretically, with 43 million other singles in America, this should be easy, but it isn't, especially in large cities. Nor is it easy when one carries around the image, as most singles do, that the world is made up entirely of married couples.

It may appear to you that this problem of meeting other singles applies primarily to young people with minimal social experience, but in actuality it involves singles of all ages and of all degrees of sophistication and experience. In fact, the never-marrieds are usually aware of where the singles are and have had a lot of practice in developing friendships, but the newly divorced or widowed, totally out of dating circulation for ten or twenty years, often have no idea how to go about meeting other unmarrieds. Since half of all singles are formerly married people, getting back into a singles social world becomes very important.

The problem may not be yours. If you have an especially interesting job or are particularly outgoing and gregarious, you may meet all the people, single and married, you care to meet, but we urge you to read this chapter anyway. You may come across a concept that hadn't occurred to you, or you may discover, as many singles do, that the problems of other singles illuminate your own, sometimes in unexpected ways.

WHAT KEEPS YOU FROM MEETING OTHER SINGLES?

How do you feel about having to "search" for other singles? Your attitude will determine both the quality of the search and the success of the outcome. If you regard the search as a natural part of your situation rather than an embarrassing aspect of your life, your chances of conducting it well are immeasurably increased.

What may be holding you back from meeting other singles is a basic confusion about why you want to meet them in the first place. Our society is so sexually obsessed that it points almost all relationships between men and women in the same direction—bed. So the phrase "looking for other singles" is inevitably sex-tinged. When you go to singles' affairs, you are obviously not looking for a guru or a transcendental spiritual experience, but neither are you necessarily looking for a bed-partner. So you shouldn't let yourself be shamed into feeling you are playing a sex game if you aren't.

Looking for other singles can mean many things: looking for same-sex friends, opposite-sex friends, companions, platonic friends, same-interest friends, just plain interesting people—even lovers or potential marriage partners, for that matter. But before we look at some of the institutions that are bringing singles together today, let's take a closer look at some of the factors that keep singles apart.

The sociological facts of life undoubtedly contribute to keeping people apart. The isolation brought on by the spread of our cities (which can result in people living miles apart) and the mobility of our society (which can result in acquaintances lost through moves and job changes) are contributory factors. It takes increased effort to keep track of friends in a mobile, urban society. However, many singles have no problem keeping up a fulfilling and varied social life. Invariably, they have overcome, or were fortunate never to have, psychological stumbling blocks of the following kind.

The Loser Syndrome

Just as many singles feel distressed going out alone, many more feel embarrassed by the fact that they are openly searching for companionship. It implies that one has somehow lost or never found, his birthright—a lifetime partner. In addition, to be out searching is seen as a pretty revealing statement about oneself. It says, "I'm available," or, "I'm lonely," or, "I'm looking for someone," depending on the degree of embarrassment.

If being single, in and of itself, is experienced as shameful or as a stigma, then there is no way that having to look for other singles can be taken as anything but proof of your inadequacy and inferiority. The underlying assumption is that if you were only more attractive, more desirable, more whatever, you wouldn't have to look at all, and prospective friends and partners would be beating at the door.

And this disparaging secret loser self-image works both inwardly and outwardly. Saddled with this mental attitude, it is impossible to win: If no one pays attention to you, it's proof you are a "loser"; on the other hand, if someone does pay attention to you, your self-image frequently is so low that you conclude this person must be a "loser" too.

The Sex-Object Syndrome

Another psychological handicap is seeing yourself as a commodity in the marketplace. One single woman said, "The idea is to look but never look like you're looking—because if you're caught looking, you automatically lose points. It's as if you're saying, 'I'm ready—take me.'" She explains, "That's why I would never go where all the singles are supposed to be—especially single bars—because that would make me feel just like a 'chunk of beef' on display."

Although many public events for singles do have a bartering, mercantile quality about them, the trouble with this attitude is its logic. No environment, no matter how unpleasant, should make you feel like anything you are not. And you have it in your ability to control this. If you repeatedly see yourself as a "chunk of meat" in a single's bar or anywhere else, it may be you actually see yourself that way in *any* encounter with the opposite sex.

If you see men as "creeps who are only after sex," no matter what an individual man does or doesn't do in your presence, sooner or later he will begin fitting into your "creep" stereotype, and you will be disappointed in him (while being secretly satisfied that your prejudice was verified once again).

The Kismet Syndrome

In a way, the opposite of this object syndrome is a tradition in our romantic mythology which says that finding someone is supposed to "just happen"; that is, one should not have to be put, or put oneself, on the auction block. This belief in kismet, or fate, is all the more beguiling because it relieves us of the necessity of having to accept full responsibility for our lives. Well, kismet helps those who help themselves—and it is high time we begin to learn to help ourselves. Besides, over the centuries kismet hasn't done all that great a job.

Meeting interesting singles doesn't "just happen"—except in rare instances. And, furthermore, it never did "just happen"—even historically. You have to take responsibility for making it happen. Somewhere between the extremes of making oneself into an object and blithely waiting for Prince or Princess Charming lies a sane middle ground.

The Rejection Syndrome

You may tell yourself consciously that you want to meet interesting singles, but unconsciously, you may be holding back and appearing aloof out of a fear of rejection. Clearly one of the strong factors that keeps us from meeting new people is the common fear that they don't want to meet us. We all know hundreds of ways to undercut a relationship, to let others or ourselves down, or, indeed, to prevent the relationship from getting started in the first place. This fear may keep you from going out at all, or you may be going through all the motions when you are with other singles with no real intention of following through. We will deal with remedies for this fear later in the chapter.

Until a few years ago, people in America tended to marry those who lived within a radius of twenty blocks of them. And in Europe, the old matchmaking customs did bring people together in what was perhaps a less chaotic way than ours. The *paseo* of Latin countries and the *promenade* of the Balkans—where, on the town plaza each Sunday afternoon, women would walk to the left and men to the right, sizing each other up and later talking—seem at least as efficient in exposing the unattached to each other as anything to be found in today's urban centers.

In pre-World War II America there was far more "community" than now. The individual is now responsible for forging out an independent life, without much community contact. An unfortunate (but predictable) effect of this change is that our new independence has outstripped the methods for bringing people together.

Just where do you go to meet interesting, compatible singles? Traditionally, church and ethnic groups, social clubs, classes, and political clubs—all are time tested and should be explored. Make up a list for yourself. However, what is crucial is not the list itself, but which item on it seems most suited to your personality.

If you are interested in intellectual pursuits, call the adult education departments of nearby colleges or high schools and see what courses they offer.

If you are athletic but have been too busy to do anything about it, or if you just think you need some exercise, call your local park or recreation department, or a coeducational spa or health club, and find out what it offers. If you like outdoor activities, try bicycle clubs, the Sierra Club and the local Y's for information on interesting groups. Once you begin looking, you will be overwhelmed by the number of ways one may pursue a particular interest.

Your attitude, though, is important. Your focus must be on what you're doing and how much you enjoy it, not on the possibility of whom you will meet. This way, you will be more relaxed and more responsive to whatever the experience brings you. You may meet no one of particular interest. Or you may meet a single of the same or opposite sex whom you will want to know better. Or you may even meet a married couple, and they may later introduce you to other singles—and then again, maybe they won't. Whether or not you meet anyone of more than passing interest, you will have become involved in an activity that gives you pleasure, in and of itself, and this is the important thing. It may seem paradoxical that "not consciously seeking" is the best way to find what you are seeking, but in actual practice this turns out to be the case more often than not.

Let us now assume that you are willing to be more venturesome and try activities and ideas that are specifically designed to bring singles together. Which should you try, and which should you avoid; which work, and which don't?

FINDING OTHER SINGLES

When you are ready for a direct attack on the singles scene, the singles group or club may be a good place to start. You will usually find a listing of such singles events and activities in the Sunday supplement of most newspapers. They include ads for singles clubs, discussion groups, lectures, workshops, encounters, dances, bars, cruises, and weekend retreats. How do you choose among them? Our answer is to try them all, or as many as possible, choosing first those that genuinely interest you.

Discussion Groups

These groups can be one of the best ways to meet others because they are smaller and more intimate, and in the give-and-take of talking, you become a part of a group, not just a witness to an event. When there, ask other singles how they manage and what groups and events they find most rewarding. A personal recommendation is worth a dozen blind guesses, and people are amazingly helpful once they know you want advice. But no one can read your mind; you have to ask first.

Singles Clubs

These clubs usually charge an annual fee and require donations at the door for specific events. They vary widely in effectiveness. Sometimes women complain that competition for men in club activities is rather fierce and that the men have learned to make the most of it. If you find yourself in a group where such contretemps make fun difficult, try changing to another group until you find one more to your own liking. Don't let one bad experience—or even a couple—turn you away.

Encounter Groups

In many cities now, there are "growth centers" which employ what has become known as the encounter method. These centers usually have workshops, discussions, weekend retreats—all dedicated to enhancing self-knowledge and social and personal skills based on techniques of liberating and expressing one's real feelings. The give-and-take of encounter is an excellent way to get to know yourself better, and is therefore of tremendous potential benefit to the single for whom individual change and growth does not present a threat.

An interesting sidelight on the encounter group is how disproportionately large singles' participation often is. Some group leaders believe that the reason for this is that individual change often represents a threat to stability in a marriage and in consequence, one or both members of a married couple "veto" participation.

One must, in point of fact, use caution in some of these groups, however, for if the leader is not well trained, the experience can be emotionally risky. On request, the Association of Humanistic Psychology in San Francisco will send you a list of professionally run growth centers in your area.

Newspaper Ads

In all probability, one of the last things in the world you would ever think to do would be to take out a newspaper ad about yourself. After all, you are not a tube of toothpaste or a second-hand car. The very thought of such a thing may seem demeaning or dangerous or both, but based on the experiences of many singles in "Challenge" workshops, you would do well to reconsider.

As many as 120,000 singles—many of whom may have once thought as you do and most of whom are not that much different from you—take out such ads each year in publications such as underground papers, metropolitan dailies, singles magazines, and even such intellectually oriented journals as the *New York Review of Books.* What is more important, many report they have had a lot of success at it.

The truth is that in an anonymous society such as ours, it is easy to feel ignored or to be ignored unless you know firmly who you are and what you want and you let others know it too. And the more directly and realistically, the better. Instead of thinking of it as "offering yourself" to a faceless horde of readers, think of it, rather, as an efficiency technique for zeroing in on the kind of person you would like to meet. One obvious advantage is the opportunity to really pick and choose among correspondents if you get enough replies.

Lucy, a bright thirty-two-year-old secondary teacher who attended a workshop, has run ads on three occasions. "It is ten times more efficient than blind dating or the introductions of friends or just chance meeting," she explains. "I simply say what I want. What could be more precise or simple? I say 'Interested in meeting a manly, considerate, intellectual with professional or artistic interests, who likes his work, the outdoors, simple things—and enjoys life.' It may sound corny, but I've analyzed what it is I admire in a man and for me, it comes down to these ingredients. Any man who gets the right vibes reading that ad is a man I would like to meet."

Some people use newspaper ads because of their very anonymity. We know of a prominent assemblyman in a Western city who wouldn't dream of meeting other singles in bars, or going to singles dances, but who does use newspaper ads, finding them not only more discreet as a means of meeting other singles, but more efficient as well.

Interestingly, running newspaper ads to meet other singles has long been an acceptable social custom in England, Sweden, and other European countries. But it has only recently become respectable in America—first, because it simply answers a new need, and second, because Americans are becoming less uptight about thier social lives.

The only way to get a feel for what newspaper ads are like is to get some of the publications and follow them closely for a few issues. Before placing one of your own, you might try answering any that look interesting. Remember that you have a number of built-in safeguards. First, you can exchange letters using a box number at the publication rather than your own home address. Then, you can check out your impression further by telephone. After these steps, you can meet the person in some comfortable public place and carry on your relationship from that point. In general, it is unwise to put your phone number and home address in an ad.

If you have the impression that most newspaper ads tend to be a come-on for kinky sex, you're wrong. Some obviously are, but it is their very obviousness which makes it fairly easy to avoid getting involved with them. One also has to give thought to the specific paper or magazine used. The more the publication is directed toward a special interest audience (particularly if it is your special interest), the more likely it is that a reply will come from someone with whom you will feel comfortable.

Of all newspaper outlets, advertising in singles newspapers is probably most effective. They vary in quality, and many singles magazines and tabloids fold almost as quickly as they go into print. The *Singles Register,* which has been publishing since 1970 and is distributed nationally and internationally, is a well-written publication, totally dedicated to filling the need of singles to meet other singles. Judging from the ad responses, it does this quite successfully.

According to the publisher, most ads draw at least thirty to forty replies, out of which informants say anywhere from four to five respondents turn out to be "highly datable." One divorcée's ad drew 168 replies recently. It read:

> Sensitive, intelligent, educated woman, 39, trim, 5'4", considered attractive, divorced. Enjoy: the outdoors, honesty, good conversation. Looking for sincere, outgoing, intelligent man who enjoys life and has a good sense of humor.

As other examples of what the ads are like, here are two which we recently clipped.

> Hi, I'm Russ. Anyone out there interested in meeting a guy 6'1", 170 lbs., 46, financially secure

insurance salesman? Non-smoker, non-drinker, love sports, movies and talking.

A woman put in this ad:

Teacher, journalist, 40, 5'4", 125 lbs. Excited about life. Open to new experiences—enjoy traveling, people, or quiet evenings. Love to read, have three pets and am a gourmet cook.

As you can see, these are straightforward ads. They are representative of a large majority of people who place such ads—direct, "normal" people who seem to know what they want and who are looking for someone who will enjoy sharing their interests with them.

One of the hidden values of giving this method some honest consideration is the opportunity it gives you to make up a statement describing how you see yourself and what you are looking for in someone else. Even if you don't place the ad, writing it can be revealing and help you to focus on what you really hope to get from a relationship.

It has become fashionable in some recent books on singles to characterize this method of meeting others as gauche and desperate. We feel, based on experience, that it isn't. We recommend it. It works, it is effective, and the experience is more grist for your risk-taking mill.

Computer and Other Dating Services

Although matchmatching has a long history in European countries, formal introduction by mail goes back only to the late nineteenth century in this country. The first venture of this sort was organized by Henry Jahn of Minneapolis, in

1891. While it never became widely successful, surprisingly enough it still exists today under the name of *Cupid's Column,* a published description of people interested in meeting other people—the object being matrimony. Another correspondence club established in this period was the Standard Correspondence Club in Grayslake, Illinois, founded in 1899 by J. W. Schlosser. It continued to operate for at least sixty years. At the turn of the century, the following ad appeared in poster form in Eastern cities under the aegis of the Halcyon Matrimonial Company of New York City.

Rates: All candidates (male and female) East of
Mississippi River $50. each
Females wishing to migrate
West of Miss. R. $25. each
Males West of Mississippi River $95. each

We've received inquiries from gentlemen of breeding who have gone West and settled in thriving communities. It is quite reliably reported that many of their homes contain indoor water pumps, are warm in winter months and offer most of the conveniences of eastern living. Shown above [in their poster picture] is a group of honest, temperate men, who dwell in a western town that has one thousand males to every female. In many cases, the gentlemen offer to pay their ladies' transportation costs over land or by ship to their new homes.

Computer dating is a modern outgrowth of these introduction services. It originated in 1965 when some Harvard undergraduates pressed an IBM 1401 computer into action, more or less as a lark, to collate and "match" a group of dating candidates. The commercial possibilities were instantly evident, and since then many computer dating services have opened their doors.

For those who feel uncomfortable about meeting people through newspaper ads or by going to any large gathering of singles, computer dating and the more traditional dating services offer another alternative. Women sometimes feel that it may be too dangerous and that they may be inundated with a flood of odd characters, but as with newspaper ads, there are the same built-in safeguards. You have a chance to sort out your impressions by letter or phone and bypass anyone who just doesn't sound "right." Before you invite anyone to your house or have a regular "date," you can meet him or her in a safe, public place. In fact, most people who go to all the trouble and expense of signing up with a dating service are serious, responsible people.

Perhaps the greatest advantage of a dating service is that it provides an arena in which to practice risk taking in meeting other singles. If you are not counting on it to find the perfect "other" for you, but rather to introduce you to reasonably compatible people who may turn out to be real friends, then your expectations are likely to be fulfilled. Look upon each computer introduction as only an experiment and not a live-or-die proposition.

However, there are some things to watch out for. Presumably, a dating service does all the prescreening for its clients, but that assumption is not necessarily true. Many "computer dating" services use no electronic equipment whatsoever, they have too few clients and too few variables for anything but a rudimentary matching which can better be done by hand. This is certainly true of some of the more expensive firms which have almost priced themselves out of clients.

For this reason, you are probably better off if you choose one of the less expensive companies of the four or five you may see advertised in the Sunday newspaper. They are certain to have many more clients, which is, of course, an essential ingredient in any effective dating service, since it takes thousands of names in order to come up with really good matches.

A frequent complaint about these services arises from the problem that people lie or "stretch facts" when they fill out the initial questionnaire. Sometimes this may be a conscious effort to deceive, but frequently it is because people are not even aware of how "wishful thinking" has become reality for them. Aside from the screening you yourself do, there seems to be no way to cope with this inherent defect.

Another problem is that computer matchmaking is a pretty impersonal affair, at least as it is done by most computer dating firms—irrespective of how highly priced they are. You fill out a questionnaire and send it in, and then you are sent a list of presumably "matched" people who may call you, or whom you may call, and that is it. There is no follow-up to see whether the clients are happy or unhappy with the services' efforts—whether or not they succeeded at all. Lost are all the many intangibles, the personal factors, the subtleties that often make all the difference in whether or not two people take to each other in a meaningful way.

A thirty-five-year-old accountant had a disappointing experience involving such an "intangible" that only personal screening could have picked up. "I had this 'match' with a librarian in her early thirties, who turned out to be a lovely girl," he said. "The only trouble was that she was a food faddist. That wouldn't have been so bad except for the peculiar way it managed to dominate our relationship.

"At the time, she was entranced by a little book, a bestseller called *Folk Medicine,* which recommended honey and vinegar as an antidote for practically everything. She had been taking this stuff daily—so much that, frankly, she simply reeked of vinegar. Her idea was that if three table-spoons were good, ten were better. It was on her breath all the time. I don't know where the honey went. I just couldn't take it, and I didn't have enough nerve to tell her about it."

You can do a little screening of the service itself on the basis of its public face. Computer dating has been guilty of its share of high-pressure advertising, which may turn you off. Recently, a San Francisco firm, which charged $475 for testing and matching, used the theme, "How much is it worth to you not to be alone anymore?" Another company took the approach, "You can't cuddle TV, or your money, or your stereo. . . ." Many people don't like to be appealed to on that level and won't go to computer firms for that reason alone. If a particular service's advertising doesn't appeal to you, you can assume with some certainty that it won't appeal to anyone you would be interested in.

Who uses computer dating services? A recent study shows that most clients (out of a sample of 240) are just beyond youth (average age, 38.8 years), have slightly higher educa-tion than the average population (38 percent had completed college), had marriage as their goal, and felt that other opportunities for meeting singles had proven inadequate. Twenty-one percent—not an overwhelming figure—said they found computer dating more satisfying than other methods. Still, the computer dating business continues, and it must be because some of those who don't fall within that 21 percent find some other value in the experience—like those dis-covered by David, a forty-eight-year-old engineer, who reported his experience in a "Challenge" workshop.

David, personable and widowed for two years, reported

that after he had paid $15 to a computer service, he was introduced to five different women, and while he did not find himself particularly attracted to any of them, he thought he had had a good learning experience.

His first date, Eileen, was an elementary school teacher. They met after dinner for dessert and coffee, and conversed pleasantly until the topic veered casually to religion. Eileen strongly believed in organized religion, both for herself and for any children she might have in the future. David, on the other hand, was an agnostic. The more they talked, the more they both saw they were hopelessly unsuited, particularly since they didn't really agree on politics or life-styles, either. He didn't see her a second time.

Afterward, David saw four other women from the computer service in quick succession. With each one, he found himself less nervous and actually looking forward to the experience—something quite new for him. More than that, he discovered his new-found skill in risk taking was actually carrying over into his work and other relationships. The "safe" path, which had been the only one he would take in personal relationships, now seemed entirely too dull.

He enjoyed his four other dates, but since he still found basic differences of viewpoint in many areas, he did not have enough interest in them to pursue the relationships further. But he got far beyond his nervousness at dating again and developed a clearer picture in his mind of exactly what kind of woman he would like to know better.

He assessed it this way: "The important thing about my computer experience is that it gave me courage to go out and try other means of meeting people. Since that experience, I have gone to a club that has singles discussion groups, and I even signed up for a singles cruise. Each experience has made me surer of myself."

Summing up, we might list the pros and cons of computer dating as follows:

PROS	CONS
Possibilities of making real friendships	Could have undesirable experiences
Help to focus on the kind of person you want to meet	Could sidetrack you from other interests and other procedures for meeting singles
Practice in social skills	If it doesn't work out, might be discouraging

Generally speaking, we think computer dating is probably worth the effort, all things considered. The pros seem to balance the cons, and like everything else, much depends on the spirit with which you use it. Tried with a spirit of adventure and with proper precautions, there seems little that can harm you in computer dating.

Singles Bars and Dances

Singles bars and dances are, for most unmarrieds, the least favorite places for meeting other singles. This is true even though a few of the newer, refurbished bars in urban centers such as New York seem to be doing well. A new singles superbar called Adam's Apple opened in New York two years ago and grossed $2 million in the first year. Business is so good that the owners envision franchising fifty similar bars in the United States and abroad during the next year or two. The owner decorated it with artificial fruit trees, a waterfall, and rustic setting so that "it doesn't seem like a singles bar, which is what a good singles bar should avoid seeming like."

These newer bars don't resemble too closely the traditional singles bars of recent years. Typically, the noise, the frenzy and shouting, the highly competitive "quick score" atmosphere of many of these bars was (and continues to be) a turn-off for many singles. The constant looking around for somebody better, the wandering gaze, the total loss of one-to-one concentration make these places anathema to many singles. By contrast, the paperwork and follow-up of a newspaper ad or computer dating services seems almost serenely personalized.

Many singles have a fixed idea that singles dances and bars are places where they are most on display as sexual "merchandise." When singles go to them, they have to face up to their embarrassment and guilt feelings at wanting to meet other singles in the first place.

A never-married man of twenty-eight confessed, "I go to a singles bar from time to time when I'm really lonely and I want to meet somebody. It's the last thing in the world I'd ever tell anybody else about. That's why it was so funny when I bumped into a single business associate of mine one night at a singles bar. I thought he had his social life all tied up with a bow knot and would never have to go to such places. We both laughed and agreed that it wasn't that easy to meet other singles."

If you saw the movie "John Loves Mary," with Dustin Hoffman and Mia Farrow, you saw the singles bar scenario—book, chapter, and verse. In it, John meets Mary (in a singles bar, of course), John goes to bed with Mary, John loses Mary, John finds and realizes he is in love with Mary, and before the curtain falls, John remembers to ask Mary her name. At that time, the movie was considered shocking, even though people did think of singles bars primarily as "body exchanges." However, this notion is changing.

Those singles dances which are still around come in all sizes, from small (thirty to forty people) to a gigantic bash for a thousand, like the one held not too long ago on the *Queen Mary*, which is permanently docked in Long Beach, California. Obviously, the chances of meeting and really getting to talk to and know other singles is better if the group is smaller. However, most singles, both men and women, find that attending singles dances leaves them feeling somehow "down-graded" and depressed—more so than singles bars—and after attending two or three, they rarely go again.

"One of the few times I have ever been really depressed as a single was at a singles dance," said a forty-two-year-old widow. "There is such desperate emphasis on looking good and seeming animated. Even if you don't want to dance with someone, you feel you have to, or you run the risk of hurting his feelings. And besides, I feel so sleazy." Men, even attractive men, often complain of the embarrassment of being rejected and the pressure of having to shop around.

One unmarried man said that in order to ask a particular woman to dance, he had to sidle by three tables of women, all observing the scene, sipping their drinks, and waiting. When she refused him, he had to pick his way back past those tables again, doubly embarrassed, because they had witnessed his public rejection and probably would refuse him if he were to ask any of them to dance, feeling they were second choice.

However, if dancing really turns you on, then by all means, the singles dance may be for you. You could then focus on the fun of dancing, in and of itself, and forget about the rest of it. With the right attitude, such dances can be fun. You may enjoy yourself even more if you go to square dances or folk dances, where the emphasis is generally on fun and dancing itself, rather than on trying to meet someone.

Singles Are Everywhere

The *Encyclopedia of Associations* contains more than 17,000 entries. The listed organizations range from star-gazers, button collectors, and walking clubs to professional clubs and associations of every description. There are madrigal societies, model railroad groups, German shorthair pointers associations, and clubs for yoga meditators, antique collectors, little theater groups, and junior symphonies. In almost every community of any size there are dozens of organizations eager for new members, but it's up to you to go out and get involved in them. You must take full responsibility for yourself.

TAKE A CHANCE–SAY HELLO

Having reviewed many ways and places you can meet other singles, we would indeed be remiss if we did not mention a basic method essential if you are to meet others: learn—force yourself if necessary—to say hello. It doesn't matter how you start the conversation, or where, if you do so directly and openly. It seems a small thing, but if you do not take responsibility for the full living of your life, then certainly no one else will.

Keep in mind that no matter how aloof and self-sufficient other singles may seem, the vast majority are just as eager to meet you as you are to meet them. Behind bravado and apparent self-confidence lurk some of the same shyness and I-don't-want-to-be-rejected fears you feel yourself. Knowing this should allow you to be bold, to be strong, to break the ice—people will love you for it, and you have nothing to lose by doing so. If the other person doesn't say hello to you, he or she is the one who is missing out. President Franklin D. Roosevelt, when asked the secret of his poise, replied, "Realizing that other people are just as afraid to speak to me—especially the first time—as I am to speak to them." With this in mind and with a willingness to approach others in a friendly way, you may be pleasantly surprised by the warm reception you get.

Try it not just at parties or singles activities, but at art galleries, museums, and zoos; people are leisurely and contemplative at such places and usually open to exchanging views once someone leads the way. Supermarkets and laundromats are other places where talking to strangers is the easy and natural thing to do. How many times have you stood in line with your basket, behind someone to whom you wanted to speak? Next time—do it.

The way to turn strangers into friends is by taking the initiative and then going more than half way toward cultivating that friendship. Eventually, you will begin to look at almost all people as potential friends, not fearful strangers.

Ralph Keyes, in his sensitive and provocative book, *We, The Lonely People—Searching for Community*, points out that "A sense of community is what we find among people who know us, with whom we feel safe. And that rarely includes our neighbors." Keyes adds: "Once the secret is out—that we all need each other—we can take a communal deep breath and begin to rebuild something we can no longer afford to attempt to live without." We profoundly agree with him and also believe that this building of community can begin right at our nearest supermarket.

A last thing that you must remember about meeting singles is that, while it may not always seem so, they are literally everywhere—43 million of them. Since there are 97 million married people, almost every third person you meet will be single—and they will be looking to meet other singles, too.

8. Sex
and Maybe Love

In our society, getting sex in perspective is no small achievement. On the one hand, since childhood many of us have
been subjected to repressive teachings that result in guilt and
embarrassment where sex or almost anything to do with the
body is concerned. In or out of marriage, few of us are able
to overcome this unfortunate upbringing completely. On the
other hand, we now live in a sex-obsessed culture that hard-
sells sex in movies, TV, and magazines, on billboards and at
the corner newsstand.

The current era of so-called permissiveness may be a long-
overdue reaction not only to Victorian repression and
hypocrisy but to centuries of sexual denial. In the long run it
may be a good thing, but because of it, most of us, in our
deepest consciousness, are caught in an emotional crossfire.
Taught to feel guilty about sex—especially sex outside of
marriage—yet exhorted to turn on to it, we are left with
anything but a clear vision of what our sex lives should be.

This legacy of confusion is especially hard for singles. They are the special victims of the moral absolute that has come down to us from centuries past: that sexual relations outside of marriage are wrong. While adjustments have recently been made in this absolute, the basic premise still holds true for a large section of the population.

Try, for example, telling a landlord unwilling to rent to a single just because he or she is single and might conceivably have a sex life—on the premises—about the new enlightenment in sexual mores. You may find yourself arguing against a stereotyped view that all singles are libertines who can't wait for the next swinging party to happen. This stereotype is eagerly clung to by those who believe sex is wrong outside marriage, who secretly envy any group or person reputed to be doing it, and who would like to strike back at the objects of their envy by damaging their reputation, labeling them licentious, or denying them respectability—and sometimes a roof over their head.

Given such a situation, it is no wonder that some singles are deeply confused and respond by throwing themselves into a frenetic pursuit of here-and-now pleasures or by trying to avoid the problem through continence. Still others launch a do-or-die search for the one-and-only, figuring it is better to marry than to burn.

Obviously, sex is more than hormones and technique, which is to say that sexual maturity is clearly much more than a matter of puberty. Perhaps this is why the current emphasis on sexuality has left us wondering perplexedly why sex doesn't always (or even often) result in the sustained joy, fireworks, exultation, and peak experiences promised us.

There are enough manuals and guidebooks about sex on the market to provide anything from basic knowledge to sophisticated enlightenment, so we will not cover any of that same ground here. Besides, while such manuals may serve the purpose of freeing us behaviorally in some respects, and while they may relieve our anxiety by telling us how other people behave, the real need for the single still lies in getting in touch with and understanding his own sexual attitudes, needs, and feelings in order to have a better idea of what to do about them.

Nor will we talk about how to cope with any medical problem such as contraception, abortion, or VD. There is plenty of literature available in those areas, too, much of it free. Inquiries can be directed to your own county health department, family planning council, or Planned Parenthood and Zero Population Growth groups.

Clearly, it is not possible for us to get anyone over his sex hang-ups by means of the written word alone. Not only do we believe that there is no one form of behavior that is right for all people, but sexual attitudes are so deeply etched into personality that changing them can be a long and difficult process.

The purpose of this chapter is rather to look at some of the sexual problems inherent in the single life and to help you put sex in perspective. It is intended to help you become realistic about your own sexual feelings and needs, whatever they may be. Our thesis is that just as it is okay to be single, it is okay to have the sexual feelings and the sex life that you choose as best suited to you as a single.

THE UNPREDICTABILITY OF SEX

Sex can be a major source of frustration in a single's life. But the single isn't alone in this: It is often a source of dissatisfaction in many married lives as well. Sometimes people are suited to each other in a lot of ways that make living together delightful, but are not compatible in bed. This may turn out to be true almost from the start of the marriage and remain so for years. Or the sexual relationship may start out well and turn bad for many reasons: deteriorating communication, economic stress, overwork, boredom, etc. A poor sexual relationship may not break up the marriage immediately—or ever—but it can remain a point of strain and weakness in the marriage that keeps it from being all it should be.

Fortunately, singles don't have the potentially terrible problem of having committed themselves to a lifetime of sex that may not suit them at all. One might think that singles, being beholden to no one and presumably "free," would have an abundant sex life of enormous variety and satisfaction. This is certainly the concept the media have promoted, and consequently it is what a lot of marrieds believe about singles and what a lot of singles believe about other singles. Those working in the singles field, however, know that by and large it just isn't so. There are many factors that preclude this from happening.

Some of them are psychological—guilt about one's sexual feelings and confusion over what one's sex life should be like are two main ones. In addition, there are the simple facts and circumstances in life that keep people apart or make good relationships difficult to establish and maintain. Some of these are the pressures of time, work, and energy, isolated urban life styles, fears and apprehensions about getting involved and the inhibiting presence of children in the homes of many singles.

All these add up to one of the most frustrating problems for singles: the sheer unpredictability of their sex lives.

Overall, singles complain that there isn't enough sex when they want it or more rarely, that there's an abundance available when they can't handle it. For most singles, it is either feast or famine. Though there may be long periods at the bare subsistence level, the sex life of singles lacks the predictability associated with marriage. And it is anything but the copulation cornucopia associated with the popular image of the swinging single.

When singles discuss these problems in "Challenge" workshops—and they do it with great interest—what emerges first is the realization that hardly anyone claims to have solved all his problems about sex or to be completely sure that his sexual attitudes are "right." Many have at least one area they regard as a major barrier to a complete sex life.

One problem comes up repeatedly in "Challenge" groups. A surprising number of singles have not really accepted the idea that it is indeed okay to have sex·outside of marriage. There is some variability according to age and experience. The newly divorced and widowed and the older never-marrieds tend to feel this way more often than younger never-marrieds. However, the problem exists even for singles who date actively and talk easily about their acceptance of sex; as the discussions become more frank and honest, they discover that their real feelings are more ambivalent than they realized.

Other problems range from the unfulfilled expectations of a few avant-gardists who desire to explore the furthest reaches of sexual freedom, to the anxieties of the equally few singles who don't want a full sex life with the opposite sex at all and feel abnormal because of it. Of course, for a certain number of singles (as for a number of marrieds), their problems are homosexual rather than heterosexual. This book is not designed to deal with homosexuality, although many of the observations in this chapter apply to gaining a fulfilling life in that community as well.

In "Challenge" workshops singles get a measure of courage

and new confidence as they learn that others share their feelings and as they see how others handle their sex lives. Just discovering that others have similar problems is a revelation to many singles and a big step forward in determining what they want to do about theirs. What clearly emerges from these discussions is that there is no ideal, problem-free sex life that fits all singles, and no single way of solving any particular problem.

The very complexity of our individual personalities and sexual drives makes it impossible to come up with any pat formula for everyone. Individuals have the most enormous variability in their sexual needs and desires. What might seem like a fulfilling sexual arrangement for one person would seem like a starvation diet to another with a stronger sex drive. But sex is not just a matter of physical drives, it is equally, perhaps even more, a result of psychological forces; consequently, in figuring out what our sex lives should be like, we must take into consideration all the varied motivations people have for engaging in sex.

SEX FOR MANY REASONS

Just as people do not always eat solely because they need the food for energy or because they enjoy good food, but instead use eating to cope with and allay any number of other emotional needs (tension, insecurity, the feeling of being unloved), similarly, sex often becomes entangled with some of the same stressful personality needs. These have little to do with the direct communication of affection, which is what most people believe sex is all about—or at least should be all about. These needs may play a part in almost any relationship, more strongly at some times than at others.

However, when they dominate a sexual relationship, they almost always cause trouble between the two people involved.

For singles, who have no marital sexual obligations and are relatively free agents in the world of interpersonal relationships, it is particularly important to be aware of what they are doing and why they are doing it. Then the elements involved in the decision to have sex with a particular partner are clear, and the "yes" or "no" of it is much easier to deal with.

In discussions with singles, the following uses of sex have been repeatedly mentioned as stumbling blocks to a good relationship:

Sex for Instant Intimacy

This attitude puts sex first in a relationship on the premise that sex automatically brings people closer together emotionally. The attitude is understandable because we have all been so brainwashed by a society that says sex can solve any and all problems that some of us begin to believe it can magically break down all barriers between two people. It therefore comes as a big (and disappointing) surprise for people to learn that physical intimacy does not mean emotional intimacy. Instant intimacy is usually involved in a one-night stand, but it can also be involved in a longer relationship that typically seems to start bogging down whenever the partners leave the bedroom.

The reason lurking behind this syndrome is that some people fear emotional intimacy far more than they fear sex, and they use sex as a replacement for intimacy. Real intimacy involves two people getting to know each other by exploring thoughts, feelings, ideas, and it takes a lot of time and talking for this to happen. It isn't easy to achieve real intimacy, and since it is so much easier to hop into bed, many people settle for the illusion of intimacy which sex can beguilingly provide—for a time.

One divorced man of forty-two said: "I felt pretty low after my divorce and wanted to meet someone I could feel close to. I thought that sex had a directness and honesty about it and that it would bring me automatically closer to whomever I was involved with. I just assumed that being in bed with a woman guaranteed that we would be close and intimate in other ways as well as sexually. It just doesn't work that way. In fact, if sex happens too soon, it is a good way of being pretty sure you may never get to know the other person. I now think that is why I put sex first on my list of priorities—it kept me from being emotionally intimate, which is what I really feared most of all."

Sex to Bring Love

This is a slightly more old-fashioned version of sex for instant intimacy. Sex has been so overemphasized that some women—though this is changing—believe that going to bed with a man increases the chances that he will fall in love with them. Their reasoning goes: If he doesn't love me for myself, he'll love me for my body, but he will love me. It's not all that likely, although plenty of men have stayed around as company for a woman who offered them sexual satisfaction if nothing else. Sex itself rarely brings love, although it has been responsible for some lovely dinners.

Sex for Reassurance

People whose primary purpose in sex is to make as many conquests as possible, without emotionally involving themselves in a relationship, are usually acting to overcome strong feelings of inferiority, to feel more attractive and desirable, and to prove their sexual adequacy. These are the ones who frequently do not maintain the relationship once the conquest is accomplished. Since the relief from the psychological stresses that create this behavior is usually short-lived, the Don Juan must continually make new conquests. Although previously almost an exclusively male behavior pattern, there are also a growing number of Donna Juanitas on the scene these days.

Sex for Self-Esteem

Since sex is so important in our society, being good at it is obviously something to take pride in. Wanting to please another person is not so much involved here as is narcissism and conceit. Followers of this course often make a fetish of sex, taking great pains to be up to date with the latest sex manuals. They treat sex basically as technique, to be appreciated as a game of skill like golf or tennis. Since sex is obviously more than mere technique, this is a sure road to disappointment.

Sex as an Expression of Hostility or Contempt

If you become involved with someone who uses sex to express hostility, you will know it soon enough. A tip-off that you are dealing with such a person is when he or she becomes angry and ridicules you if you refuse to go to bed with him/her right away (favorite attacks are that you're frigid or that you're not a real woman—or that you're impotent or "queer"). In any case, a person who brings these attitudes to your bed is acting out long-standing angers which have nothing to do with you and which can do a lot of harm if you let them.

Sex as a Weapon

When men or women are especially attractive and sex-oriented, they have a great opportunity to use sex as a tool for power—not just power over another person, but to gain status, money, jobs, whatever. This is rarely a masculine trait, but girls are still taught to use their "feminine wiles" to gain favors from men. There are women who, as if they learned these early lessons too well, cannot relate to the opposite sex in any other way except in these manipulating terms.

And there are other ways sex can be used for devious reasons. Sex can be used to allay tension and anxiety unrelated to sex, as an antidote to boredom, as a payment of gratitude, or as a simple biological function, seemingly without emotional content. However, all these have one thing in common: None of these distortions of real sexuality is apt to bring true sexual fulfillment.

GUIDELINES FOR YOUR OWN SEX LIFE

What, then, does bring real sexual fulfillment? What is the most rewarding sexual behavior for a single person? As we have said, there is no way anyone can answer this question for everyone. Nor is there agreement among singles about what the answers are. But even so, we can put together from what singles have said, and from what we believe, a few very broad guidelines.

Seek a Greater Awareness of Your Own Feelings

What are you using sex for? Are you acting solely out of needs like the ones mentioned above? Are you avoiding your feelings by trivializing sex, acting as if it weren't important?

Are you acting out insecurity, hostility, fear of intimacy, or any other feelings that shouldn't be a part of sex?

Perhaps you are doing none of these. But most singles discover sometime in the course of life that these pitfalls exist and are something to be wary of. Fortunately, as a single, you will probably find that your attitudes can constantly be adjusted to your changing life situation. You will be your own best teacher once you learn to trust yourself. Making decisions about your sexual conduct is something no one else can do for you. No one else has had your experiences (or lack of them), your responses, your needs, your sensitivities.

Decide What Your Sexual Threshold Is

In discussing sexual relations, most singles in "Challenge" workshops say that they are interested in sex only when it is with someone for whom they feel affection. Some others say that strong physical attraction is enough, and when they find someone with whom the "chemistry" is right, sex is natural and okay, whatever the state of emotional intimacy between them.

The point is that you are the final arbiter on these matters, and you should not allow peer-group pressure, social mythology, or the demands of another to compromise your own best judgment. Know yourself and stick by what you believe.

One widow of fifty-two found herself falling easily under the influence of a close friend of her own age, a woman who had been widowed for some eight years. "Oh come on, Agnes, you're just too darned old-fashioned," her friend implored in trying to get her to loosen up a little in her sexual behavior. "You know the world has changed—nobody behaves the way you do anymore." Agnes listened and against her own judgment had a brief and unfulfilling affair with a man she would not otherwise have gone to bed with. For her, sex still had to have some special feeling or commitment behind it.

"I never felt so frigid," she told a widow's group at a "Challenge" workshop, feeling somehow inadequate and a failure. "What made you think it would work?" asked another widow. "Did you think you would get over all your past training overnight? And besides, what is so great about just jumping into bed with someone anyhow? What made you so sure you were wrong?"

The thought that she might be right had just never occurred to Agnes. She just automatically assumed that since everyone else seemed to be so casual about sex, there had to be something wrong with her for not feeling that way, too. She resolved that peer-group pressure was not going to dictate her life. She would have to hack out and follow her own rules.

Be Open and Honest with the Opposite Sex

Once you understand what your feelings are in a relationship, particularly your sexual feelings, the next step is to let the other person know what they are. Obviously, this isn't always easy or even possible to do. Sometimes your feelings may be mixed or unclear. If they are, try to talk them out. The talking will help clarify them and help your partner understand you better.

Whatever the feelings may be—for example, you want to go to bed with someone but not at the moment, or you want to say no but don't want to hurt someone's feelings, or you are worried about seeming sexually inadequate, or you are afraid of getting VD, or you are concerned about getting too involved too soon—talking it out is infinitely better than playing games to maneuver or stall the other person.

When you talk, you earn the respect of the other person, you feel good about yourself, and whether or not the relationship continues, it has been put on a good basis. If sexual relations do take place, they are probably going to be better, under these circumstances, than if you hadn't talked at all.

Ken, a never-married thirty-two-year-old, had a three-year sexual relationship with Janet, for whom he cared deeply. He was shaken and depressed for some time after she was killed in an auto accident. Some months later he met Carole and started dating her even though he couldn't forget Janet.

It was Carole who first indicated her desire to have sexual relations, but Ken said, "Look, I'm just not ready for an emotional involvement. You're very attractive, and a sexual relationship could easily grow into a close, intimate relationship that I'm just not up to handling at this point in my life." Then he told Carole about Janet and the fatal car accident. The conversation cleared the air. Carole did not feel rejected and ultimately a sexual relationship did develop when Ken was ready. Any explanation other than the truth would probably have spelled a quick end to what became a meaningful friendship.

Don't Let Sex Dominate Your Life

It is imperative not to give sex an overvalued, exaggerated position if you wish to avoid the inevitable frustration that results from this distorted view. However important sex may be, it is not the single most important thing in life; it is not the end-all and be-all of every relationship between two people; you won't die if you don't have it every time you want it; and you may even choose not to take it when it is offered. Just as the lack of it shouldn't dominate your thinking, having it shouldn't be seen as the promised land, either. It isn't.

If we are conditioned to think we need something, we can feel desperate if we don't have it. If we think we need three meals a day, we can seriously believe we will slowly starve to death if we eat only two. Actually, we can thrive on only two meals a day or possibly even one if we have to.

In the same way, we can be conditioned into believing we need a certain kind of sex life. We may be convinced that two times a week is normal and therefore necessary. We may want a certain kind of sex life, but we don't need it. We may want very much to be sexually close to a certain man or woman, but we don't need to be. Not having something or someone that we really want can cause a lot of pain—the trick is to allow ourselves to experience feelings but not be overwhelmed by them. Sex may be nice, it may be wonderful, it may be utterly fantastic, or it may not be. However you view it, you should be careful not to give it a position of such dominance in your life that you fail to distinguish between your sex life and the rest of your life.

COMMON SEXUAL PROBLEMS OF SINGLES

When singles are open and honest with each other in the singles workshops, they frequently discuss certain questions and topics over and over again. The very fact that they arise so often in a discussion is certain evidence that there is no one best way to handle any of them. What you do about them will depend upon your personality, temperament, and values, but sharing the experiences and findings of other singles is what this book is all about.

What to Do about a Strong Sexual Attraction That Doesn't Involve Love and Leads to What Is Usually Described as a "One-Night Stand"

Certain singles insist that sexual attraction is reason enough for two people to go to bed together. They also contend if the attraction doesn't involve love immediately, it may soon—if it is going to. Others insist that to be sexually involved with anyone for whom there is no feeling of affection isn't something they feel right about doing. The subject is important since singles must face the whole matter of new relationships with or without various degrees of affection and/or love much more often than any other segment of society.

In general, most singles don't want one-night stands as a steady diet. They find them unsatisfactory and frustrating. They are more interested in having what they call "meaningful" on-going relationships. However, some small percentage of one-night stands that occur from time to time—occasionally on trips, under special circumstances, and depending on your attitude, your situation, and the other person—can be illuminating, memorable, or just pleasurable. The problem is in that low percentage.

The consensus seems to be that brief encounters in a romantic setting or those that happen spontaneously have the best chance of being rewarding. Those that come out of a dogged search or out of pure frustration have the least chance of being worth the trouble. Unfortunately, most one-night stands are the result of the latter.

There are obvious physical hazards—such eventualities as VD and even today, in spite of the pill, pregnancy. There is an emotional hazard as well. It is possible to become involved with another person in a remarkably short time. Saying good-bye can be quite a wrench, especially if you want the affair to continue and there are reasons why it cannot. The aftermath of such an encounter can range from depression to a considerable upset in your life.

Why Do So Many Men Want to Go to Bed with a Woman on the First Date?

Men have always chased and frequently followed women into the bedroom, but what has recently changed dramatically is the time span: what often took several months or more in the past has now been telescoped into a single day or night for many.

Some men insist on this instant intimacy just to make certain—subconsciously if not in some other way—that the relationship never gets anywhere. What they are really avoiding is emotional closeness, which is more frightening to them than physical closeness.

Obviously, aside from a strong physical attraction, many of the reasons for sex outlined earlier in this chapter play an important part. Additionally, many men feel that it is expected of them, and making the compulsory pass is more of a reflex than a genuine statement of interest.

Some women, of course, don't mind at all, provided they are strongly attracted to a man. Others do mind and feel insulted or at least annoyed when they are invited to partake of "instant sex." These same women are often the very ones who ask, after four or five weeks of dating, "I wonder what's wrong with him?" or "I wonder what's the matter with me?" if the man hasn't made a pass by then.

The men in America are not having an easier time of it than the women. Usually, they feel they are expected to act a little bit like Don Juan, and they believe that women are disappointed when they don't. They are often surprised in singles workshops to find that this is not true and that an honest discussion early in the relationship clears the air immeasurably, leaving the door open for whatever relationship is to follow.

If you are attracted to a man but you don't want to go to bed with him on the first date and you tell him so as clearly and directly as you can, and he still doesn't understand or call back—we wonder if you have really lost much after all. You may feel a little rejected at first, but he is probably someone who is not for you.

Women's liberation notwithstanding, tradition role playing cannot be reversed overnight. Since sex roles are no longer defined as they were just a few years ago, there is confusion for everyone. With traditional courtship patterns changing—a less extended pursuit, less clearly defined rules, the dropping of coyness and game playing—we often find men and women equally confused and uncertain. However, nothing prevents men from continuing to follow the old pattern of pursuer, though they may occasionally find themselves accused of treating women as sex objects if their behavior seems too self-serving.

Why Do Many Men Abandon Relationships Immediately after They Have Gotten onto a Sexual Level?

Many women complain about this. It is apparently one of the ways women experience rejection most acutely. Because the "rejection" follows so closely in the wake of the sexual encounter, it can easily re-arouse feelings of guilt and anxiety about sex itself—almost as if one were being punished for having or showing sexual feelings. It can also trigger some deeply buried self-condemnatory notions most women have had bred into their psyche, i.e., that they are no longer regarded as "nice" or "respectable" because they have slept with someone. This is all the more reason why single women should try to be as honest with themselves as they are with others—difficult as both may be. If you know what you want and why you behave as you do, then how someone else reacts to you becomes less important.

It would, of course, be very nice if relationships always grew closer, but you can't really control anybody else's behavior but your own. There may be a number of reasons why a man does not call back—some having nothing to do with you at all. For example, (1) he could already be involved in another relationship and not have told you about it; (2) he could be married and not have told you that, either; (3) he may not have enjoyed himself very much; (4) he may have enjoyed himself so much that he couldn't face the prospect of an emotional involvement; or (5) he could be emotionally immature and the Don Juan role of hopping from bed to bed may be all he can handle.

If you are really curious, you can always call him up and ask him point-blank. It may be a little difficult at first, but it is often done these days. Such a call helps clear the air, makes you feel good about yourself for taking the risk, and gives you a first-rate lesson in taking responsibility for yourself.

Why Does a Woman Lead a Man on by Indicating That She Likes Him and Then Refuse to Have Sex, Even after Dating a Fairly Long Time?

Almost all men complain about feeling rejected in a situation like this. And there is probably no way of avoiding this feeling altogether (unless you stop seeing women). It might help you to understand your own feelings if you make a deliberate effort to comprehend exactly what is going on in the woman's mind. She may say no because (1) she wants to get to know you a lot better; (2) she has strong moral, religious, or other scruples about sleeping with someone outside of marriage; (3) she may be reacting against the time-honored passive role of females; (Many women nowadays are more self-aware than they used to be and they feel, for their own self-respect, that they have as much right to "call the shots" as a man. It doesn't make you one whit less a man, or her one whit less a woman, if you acknowledge and talk out some of this cultural confusion, should it happen to be reflected in your relationship.) (4) she may also be using sex in one of the many ways we discussed earlier with special emphasis on the satisfaction that the power to grant or deny sex affords many women; (5) she may like you very much and not be attracted sexually—if so, she will probably give you an explanation if you ask her for one.

Your best bet is to talk the situation over with her honestly so that you won't imagine things that don't exist in your relationship. If she is someone you really value, then continue to see her; otherwise, accept the fact that not everyone can love you. There are others who can—and will.

What to Do When There Is a Good On-Going Sexual Relationship and One Party Wants It to Be "Exclusive," but the Other Does Not

Today, more and more people are opting for a freer relationship than the one-to-one commitment. But if you honestly feel you can't cope with the insecurity of the arrangement, then this alone may determine the end of the relationship. You undoubtedly will find plenty of other people who share your view that the one-to-one commitment is the most emotionally satisfying one.

If, on the other hand, you can stand a little risk taking, you may find that you, too, enjoy the freedom that comes with a little easing up of the "steady" relationship. There is a general agreement on one point: You should stick to your beliefs, whatever they are. You should not, indeed you cannot, insist that your partner comply with your beliefs, and if a disagreement can't be resolved, the relationship will certainly come to a quick termination anyway.

How Do Men Feel about Women Making the First Sexual Approach?

It appears from "Challenge" workshop discussions that most men still want to be the initial aggressor (indeed, our society has programmed this into males as they are growing up). However, some men say they are turned on by a woman taking an aggressive role in lovemaking. By taking the initiative, of course, a woman may relieve a shy man of the fear of being rejected, when fear is the major inhibitor of his own aggressiveness. Since it is now more culturally acceptable for a woman to take the initiative, if you are strongly inclined, try it. A little sensitivity to your partner will quickly tell you how he is reacting.

If you are a man and the idea of a woman coming on strong sexually with you seems threatening and makes you uncomfortable, you should examine exactly what it is that is disturbing you and see if you can't loosen up. It would be healthier all around if the stereotyped role behavior could be dropped and people could act as they feel, not as they are told to.

Three other topics—celibacy, masturbation, and living together—are of such interest to singles that we have devoted the next three sections of the chapter to them.

CELIBACY

Sex is sold like any other product, and you are told that if you're not consuming your share there's something wrong with you. Well, the fact is that appetites for sex vary greatly, and many of the emotional traumas that bring the previously married into the single world are apt to inhibit their sexual hungers, at least for awhile. The prevailing idea is that normal sex is lots of sex, that good sex is also lots of sex, and that the only thing worse than bad sex is no sex at all.

It is important to know, if you are in a period of voluntary or involuntary abstention from sex, that celibacy is something that one may return to (and depart from) several times in a lifetime without any ill effects whatsoever. If you are worrying that your sex drive may be diminishing because you don't want sex and haven't for months, or that your drive will disappear entirely if you don't have it soon, you can put those concerns to rest.

Many singles report that returning to regular sexual activity after a period of abstinence brings new meaning and joy to sexual activity. Once they get over the attitude of "I should be having more sex" and substitute their own feelings and desires, they are able to live without frequent sex partners and without a sense of guilt for not being a sexual consumer.

One of the quickest ways to regain a balanced view of the subject is to find out how others—real people, not the media versions—lead their sex lives. Early in the history of the "Challenge" workshops it became evident in discussions on sex that many people had secret worries about their own periods of celibacy ("Am I abnormal?" "Is there something wrong with me?"), but they were totally unaware that almost everyone in the group felt exactly the same way.

For example, widows often report that they abstain from sexual relations for many months, and sometimes even for years, after the death of their spouse because they feel they should be faithful to his memory. This reaction is confirmed in sociologist Paul Bohannan's book, *Divorce and After.* In it, he reports that one-fifth of the widows and one-tenth of the divorcees experience more than three years of abstinence before resuming sexual relationships.

Divorced and widowed men report in "Challenge" workshops that they have sexual relations somewhat sooner, but in a large number of instances the periods without sex with another person are fairly extended. In almost every case the men worry that they may have lost the capacity to feel or to perform sexually—under any circumstances.

But for anyone—divorced, widowed, separated, never-married—going through a period of abstinence, usually one good sexual relationship with a caring person quickly turns their doubts about sexual adequacy and worries about a lifetime of celibacy into a feeling of "I'm really okay after all." It happened this way with Diane, a thirty-seven-year-old divorcée:

After twenty years of marriage, Diane was terrified that she simply wouldn't know how to behave as a single woman, but she was eager to begin a new life. She suffered from extremely low self-esteem, as so frequently happens after a divorce, and she was full of fear of contact with the opposite sex after so much time spent in the insularity of marriage. On the other hand, she was still a very much alive woman full of longings and appetites whetted by her new freedom. For Diane, the strains of these conflicts were so great that it was six months before she even wanted to go out with anyone.

When Diane finally had an affair with a man she was dating, she discovered to her enormous satisfaction she was not as terrified as she had expected to be. Before Diane met the man she finally decided to marry, she went through a number of different stages. At one point she found herself playing the field, getting closely involved with a number of men at the same time—something she thought she would never do. She then became celibate once more, this time for almost a year—again, something she thought she would never do. Each experience gave her respect for the flexibility and resiliency of her personality and for her ability to manage her own life.

She now deplores (along with us) the fatuous statements in some books she has read, such as David Reuben's *Any Woman Can,* which tyrannize older women into marriage with the threat that they will deteriorate emotionally and sexually if they remain single and celibate too long. She found that it just didn't happen to her and that she bounced back each time with the same intensity, and a bit more maturity besides.

Men, too, worry about "drying up" emotionally and physically during long periods of celibacy. Forty-year-old Barry was divorced for six months and had gone out with several women but didn't feel attracted to any. He was worried about his ability to relate to women at all until he met someone who really appealed to him. "She liked me, too," he said, "and maybe that was part of it. Whatever it was, I found that the right circumstance, time, and person makes all the difference. Far from being impotent—my sexual relations are better now than during my marriage."

It is not just the divorced and the widowed singles who go through fairly long periods without sexual partners. Many never-married singles do, too. It's not the kind of thing people generally are proud of, but in workshop discussions it is something they will admit to once they see that celibacy is nothing to be ashamed of.

For some, moral considerations are the basis for the

celibacy; for others, psychological factors dominate. Certainly there are dozens of reasons why someone might not pursue a sexual partner.

It is almost impossible, for some marrieds (especially those with an envious eye) to believe that anyone like Jim—an attractive thirty-year-old never-married single—would not grab at the opportunity to bed down with a different girl friend every night of the week. "Except," says Jim, "it's not what I want. I'm just not that kind of a guy. I'm not happy jumping from person to person. I'm perfectly willing to take my time till I meet someone who really matters to me. In fact, I've gone from six months to a year without going to bed with anyone. That may seem incredible to someone who thinks about sex all the time, but it can happen. Lots of men are discriminating. Contrary to popular opinion, all single men are not led around by their gonads."

Barbara, a personable forty-year-old secretary who has been mainly celibate for a year and a half, admits it isn't her favorite state, but she has discovered she is far happier having sex only occasionally with a man she knows and feels close to rather than taking advantage of more impersonal but available liaisons.

Whatever the reasons, if the reality of your life is that you are celibate, it does not mean that you are frigid or impotent or on your way to becoming either one. You should accept this fact and let yourself know it is okay not to be having sex (just as it is okay to be single, okay to be lonely when you're lonely, okay to go out alone, etc.). And just because you are celibate at a certain period of your life doesn't mean you necessarily always will be.

But even if celibacy turns out to be a more or less permanent condition, as Kinsey's *Sexual Behavior in the Human Male* showed about prisoners, people can abstain from sexual intercourse for long periods of time and still show no ill effects. Whether you are a man or a woman, it is mostly a matter of adapting to the facts of a situation. And one such adaptation is the topic we discuss next.

SEX WITH YOURSELF

What do you do with your sexual drives when you are not involved in a close relationship and there is no likelihood of one on the horizon? When this question comes up in "Challenge" workshops, the answers range from "I take a cold shower," or "I take a fast walk," or "I play a hard game of tennis," to a hesitant, "I masturbate."

Sex is not the easiest subject to discuss in a group, but there is much less hesitancy in talking about sexual relationships with other people, or even celibacy, than in talking about masturbation. Most singles, in fact, voice distinct dislike for the word "masturbation," saying it has a negative connotation for them. Even terms like "self-pleasure," "autoeroticism," "self-manipulation," or even "sex with yourself," which many prefer, still carry a certain amount of guilt.

This guilt is hardly surprising in the light of the large and ancient legacy of sexual taboos we all carry around. Both Judaism and Christianity traditionally have ferociously proscribed masturbation, insisting that any form of sexual activity should be for the purpose of reproduction alone. In fact, it surprises many people to learn that for many centuries, masturbation was considered the first cardinal sin by the medieval Church, outranking fornication and adultery. And in orthodox Jewish codes, masturbation constitutes a major sin. At times in Jewish history it was punished by death.

With this as a legacy, it is hardly surprising that the guilt has endured and that most people, younger as well as older, have a painful and difficult struggle accepting the fact that masturbation is natural sexual behavior and for most singles, one they indulge in. The guilt persists despite the fact that, culturally, the pendulum seems to have swung the other way with the best-selling authors "J" and "M," in their books *The Sensuous Woman* and *The Sensuous Man,* recommending it highly as a way to develop and keep "the love muscles" flexible.

Still, most adults past thirty obviously find it difficult to talk about masturbation, and even the adolescents of our enlightened 1970s have trouble talking about it, too. Social psychologist Robert Sorensen, in his recent book *Adolescent Sexuality in Contemporary America,* finds thirteen- to nineteen-year-olds quite defensive and reticent when the topic of masturbation is brought up. Indeed, some feel questions in this area are a definite "intrusion," and it seems it is much easier for them to do it than talk about it, which may be a reflection of guilt.

If a man or woman has a nocturnal orgasm, this is felt to be okay, a physiological and "natural" occurrence, over which few people feel any guilt. Many people, by the way, don't realize that women have nocturnal orgasms. (Kinsey reported in his monumental studies of male and female sexuality a quarter century ago that 37 percent of females had sex dreams with orgasm, while 70 percent had sex dreams which may have included orgasm; 83 percent of males had sex dreams with orgasm, while nearly 100 percent had sex dreams which may have included orgasm.)

The basic fact is that almost everybody masturbates at some time or times during his or her adult life. Kinsey's studies showed that 92 percent of the total adult male population masturbated. Interestingly, of this figure 89 percent of those who had only gone through grade school masturbated, while 96 percent of those with a college education did. His figures are confirmed by earlier studies in the United States—from 1918 to 1947—as well as by European studies which show a similar incidence of masturbation in males (from 85 to 96 percent).

Kinsey's figures for adult women were lower: 62 percent masturbated. One might well believe that the percentage would have been higher but for a double standard which had women of that period feeling even more guilty about sex than men. Indeed, Masters and Johnson, in *Human Sexual Inadequacy*, mention increased incidence of masturbation in women from fifty to seventy and suggest it is due to increased "psychosocial freedom to enjoy masturbatory relief." The pattern seems to be that women who remain single tend to continue masturbation throughout their lives, while older women whose husbands are in failing health, or who are widowed or divorced, resume or increase their masturbation practice as time goes on.

Sometimes singles who accept the fact of their own masturbation as something that is all right have anxieties about the matter of frequency. They feel that a certain amount is okay but more than that becomes wrong. Actually, this is just another way of expressing the same old guilt. Without getting side-tracked by this issue, and assuming deep-seated guilt is a more or less constant factor in some singles (and marrieds, too), no matter what their sexual behavior, there is tremendous variation in the masturbatory practices of singles.

A twenty-two-year-old never-married man said, "Twice a week is okay but three times a week would be too much," to which a forty-seven-year-old divorced woman said, "Well, I do it every day after I shower, and I don't think that's too much. But twice a day would be too much." And there are always some who say—like a thirty-eight-year-old widow—"I just don't masturbate at all. I wouldn't feel right about it. I'd rather wait till I find someone I care about."

Kinsey's studies of male and female unmarrieds found that female singles, of all ages, masturbated on the average of once every two and a half to three weeks, while male singles masturbated on average about once a week. These are average figures, of course, and many singles, men and women, masturbate several times a week. The greater variability among the single woman is interesting—from an extreme of ten or more times within an hour (obviously related to the female's greater ability to have orgasms in rapid succession) to once or twice a year or not at all.

While the male starts to masturbate sooner and masturbates more often than the female earlier in life, the frequency declines steadily after his early twenties. Again, this is a general figure, and men obviously vary widely in their sexual drive, depending on their health, habits, life circumstances, and general outlook.

Understandably, Kinsey's studies show that the unmarried masturbate more frequently than married people. It will surprise many singles, who may have never thought about it before, to learn that most married people masturbate, too. In fact, Kinsey's figures show that the average married man masturbates once a month, while the average married woman masturbates once every three weeks, which means, of course, that some masturbate much more frequently, some less, and some not at all.

Because marrieds are expected to find total sexual satisfaction with their partner, and because they may feel that they are denying a part of their sexual responsiveness to their partner, those who masturbate usually feel a greater sense of guilt than singles. But the point that should not be lost to singles is that, whatever the situation, the mere presence of a sex partner—in marriage or out—does not automatically solve all one's sexual problems. People are extremely complex entities, and their sex lives are correspondingly complicated. It should be obvious that there is no one perfect situation, arrangement, adjustment, sex life, or partner who, at all times and in all places—and particularly, till death do us part—can fulfill all our needs, dreams and desires.

Since this is true for marrieds, how much truer is it for singles? And so we are back where we started from, but perhaps with a bit more perspective. People masturbate because it is a human thing to do, especially when they have sexual feelings that build up and there is no one with whom to express them. People masturbate because they have tensions, desires, drives—and because it is pleasurable and natural.

Because most people start to masturbate as children, we frequently grow up associating self-stimulation with immaturity. This means that in addition to having to deal with a generalized guilt about masturbation, we are also burdening ourselves with a specific guilt which says, "You are childish and immature or you wouldn't be doing this." Masturbation, however, is recognizable as universal among both males and females, from the youngest child to the oldest adult, and should not be viewed, per se, as immature behavior.

Fortunately, we rarely hear any more the old idea that the "solitary vice" (as it was once called) causes one to go crazy, or paralyzes one's hand, or brings on an attack of warts, or any of a dozen other horrors that many of us were once solemnly warned about. It is now known that it is not physically harmful in any way. Both Kinsey's and Masters and Johnson's work confirms that no physical damage comes from masturbation—regardless of frequency.

It is probably impossible to write with sufficient reassurance on this subject to convince those who have always felt guilty that they should feel guilty no longer. The facts have been known and publicized for some time, and still the same distressing feelings are aroused. In the end all one can hope for in this matter is that in the future society will be less sexually repressive and people will grow up with a more realistic view.

LIVING TOGETHER

For some singles, living together appears to offer an attractive alternative to the unpredictability that so frequently characterizes their sex lives. Whether or not you choose this course is a decision only you can make. We are not placing any moral judgment on this arrangement, but we do want to point out some long-range consequences that you may not have thought of. Because of the publicity surrounding a number of prominent couples who are living together, we have easy access to a glamorized version of this life-style, but we hear very little about the hard facts of how it usually works out. Almost nowhere do we find a realistic analysis of the disadvantages and complications involved.

Motivations and Advantages
The motivations that lead people to live together are apparent in many instances—at least to the singles involved. In the first place, one or both of the parties usually believe they are in love and they want to be together to satisfy the strong emotional hunger they feel. In addition, there is almost always a strong sexual attraction and a desire for an exclusive relationship.

There are undeniable practical advantages in such an arrangement. It is clearly cheaper and more convenient than attempting to maintain two households. All one's clothes and possessions are in one place, thus saving a lot of time, energy, and money.

Then there are certain experiential benefits. When two people are quite sure in advance that they want to get married, living together can serve as a useful prelude to, and rehearsal for, marriage. There is a greater opportunity to find out what a person is "really" like. If they are suitable, they can go ahead and get married; if they are not suitable, they can break up without any legal hassles.

There are, of course, real pleasures in such an arrangement: the closeness and honeymoon quality; the hours spent together; the availability of your lover; the simplicity of a shared social life—and many more.

Complications and Disadvantages

There is no quarrel with the admitted joys in such an arrangement, so long as it works. It may work for you, it has, and is still, working for some, but it doesn't work for most in the long run.

It is very easy to kid yourself, especially in the beginning, about what it is you are doing and why. The main complications are psychological, but there are plenty of economic, legal, and day-to-day situational problems as well. They all have to do with telling yourself you are unmarried, when to all intents and purposes, you are locked into a form of marriage. This may be okay if you understand that this is what you are doing. It is clearly not okay if you delude yourself with the belief that you are still single—and free. You are not.

You have significantly moved out of the single state. In

one way or another, you have given up the opportunity to see other people, date other people, come and go when you please, make your own decisions, choose your own friends, and pursue your own goals. In other words, you have all the restrictions of being married, but few of the advantages: lower income taxes, lower insurance rates, better chance for jobs and promotions, and a number of legal protections.

If you are in the first honeymoon glow of such an arrangement, you may be saying to yourself that the emotional closeness in living together far outweighs the disadvantages. But take a longer perspective. Such arrangements are usually short-lived. They lead to marriage or they break up in a remarkably short time (from a year to a year and a half is the average duration). And it is much harder to get out of a relationship of this sort than to get into it. This often comes as a surprise to people who have told themselves that they are really free to come and go as they wish. If it does not work out, the emotional trauma of the separation can be as wrenching as any divorce.

In an effort to avoid the pain of breaking up, some couples drift into marriage in spite of not being particularly suited to each other. Practically, it is often easier to get married than to find a way out. In many cases, their lives and possessions are so intertwined that it almost becomes necessary to first get married in order to get divorced.

The pressure to get married is liable to be especially strong if the girl gets pregnant. The fact that you are living together with someone means that you will inevitably feel more "married." Therefore, if pregnancy should occur, there is a greater push toward marriage than if you were living alone under your own roof.

Guilt is another complication. Even though you may be quite sure that this does not apply to you, once you are in the arrangement, you may be surprised by your reactions. Despite our so-called sexual enlightenment, society misses few chances to express its disapproval. Apartment managers may question you sharply about whether or not you are married, and neighbors and acquaintances may look at you quizzically.

It is especially awkward if parents know of your arrangement. Most couples try to keep their parents from knowing, which means they get involved in lying (which rarely works) or have to face a confrontation.

There can be legal complications that couples who are living together are rarely aware of until it is too late. For example, a woman works to put her boyfriend through college, supporting him for three or four years. On graduation he gets a good job, and they buy a house, car, and furniture on money he receives from his new job. A year later they decide to terminate their relationship. The woman finds to her dismay that she has no legal rights to any of the personal property acquired with the man's earnings. If they had been legally married, she would have been entitled to half. Despite the fact that she supported him all through college, she may have no legal claim to anything except a few items of personal clothing.

Another legal complication can occur if one of the partners of the arrangement dies. Except in the very few states which recognize common law marriages, if no valid will was made before death, the survivor is treated as a stranger and cannot inherit anything from the partner, even community property. Relatives of the deceased may be able to inherit even that half that should belong to the survivor.

Summing up, living together may seem like the most natural, easy thing in the world, but it can be a very complicated matter. If you ignore this fact, you do so at considerable risk. And the price you may pay for this may be greater than you bargained for. In a way, living together can be even more hazardous than getting married, because if you get married, presumably you are prepared and you know what you are doing.

If in spite of doubts and your own better judgment, you are still strongly inclined to live with someone, it might be well to consider why you are unable or unwilling to say no to such an arrangement.

One of the reasons may be that you are unable to separate the roles that sex and love have played in your motivation. Women traditionally have had to make themselves believe they were in love before they could allow themselves to have sexual relationships. This attitude has been responsible for the willingness of women through the ages to give up through marriage almost everything, including their very identities and independence, for what they thought was love but in fact may have been nothing more than the justification for a strong sexual attraction, a desire for security, the need to get away from their parents, a fear of being lonely, or one of the hundreds of other reasons for which people get married. Men, too, have felt that they should simulate love or at the very least hold out the promise of love in order to convince a woman to have a sexual relationship with them. The confounding of sex with love still permeates our cultural milieu to a large extent.

How to Make Living Together Less Hazardous

If you feel that living together is something you still want to do, in spite of all these considerations, here are some suggestions for making it less hazardous to you as a single.

First of all, talk out clearly in advance the kind of arrangement you and your partner want to have, and be very explicit. How much will each of you contribute financially and toward what will it go? How much freedom will each of you have, personally and socially? Will you date other people, see other people, have friends of the opposite sex? What areas of your life will you share, and what areas will be your own? What decisions will you make together, and what decisions alone? Who will do the dishes, the cooking, the marketing, the house cleaning?

Try to keep a little "space" in the relationship by taking a few weekends or vacations apart. If possible, maintain a separate apartment where you can have moments of solitude and privacy as an antidote to too much togetherness. This will help you preserve a little of the freedom of being single. For when you are living with someone, you are giving away your most priceless asset as a single—your freedom. Just what this freedom can and should mean to you we examine in the next chapter.

9. Freedom —The Greatest Advantage of Being Single

I take thee to be my wedded wife (husband) to have and to hold from this day forward, for better, for worse, for richer, for poorer, in sickness and in health, to love and to cherish till death us do part.

These familiar words from the marriage vow are a statement of the single most important factor of that relationship—total commitment to another person. Marriage, at its best, has this wonderful strength going for it.

In contrast, you who are single are committed to only one person—yourself—and so you can fully utilize the single life's greatest asset: freedom. A forty-eight-year-old divorcée, recently extricated from a miserable twenty-year marriage, defined it this way: "Freedom, to me, is the right to care about myself—to be what I want to be, do what I want to do, say what I want to say, and not have to 'pretend' for anyone."

We hardly need point out that she didn't define freedom in terms that would get her a passing grade in an ethics class. But she knows what is making her feel fulfilled at this point in her life—being single again after releasing herself from the confines of a bad relationship.

Of course, freedom is purely a theoretical asset unless one knows how to make the most of it. In "Challenge" workshops we find again and again that just as very few of us use more than a small percentage of our mental or creative capacity, very few singles exercise more than a little of their potential freedom. No one can be absolutely free, but we can increase manyfold the amount of freedom which we exercise.

In this chapter we steer clear of abstract definitions and discuss in practical, concrete terms how singles can use their freedom as they make decisions (whether these choices relate to mundane domestic affairs or to long-range planning of personal and professional lives). We would like to isolate some of the thoughts, actions, and attitudes which promote personal liberty and, as we shall see, help one to grow personally as a result of that freedom.

RUTS—SELF-DUG AND OTHERWISE

We all know the enormous lengths to which people will go to avoid exercising their options. All these avoidance techniques seem to involve the refusal to see significant alternatives to the way in which we are living. We pretend that our hands are tied, that we are victims of circumstances, and we settle into habitual ways of living—ruts—which make us slaves of our past.

Friendship Ruts

Do you continue to base your social life on relationships that have ceased to grow or bring pleasure? Just because close contact was rewarding once doesn't mean it will be rewarding forever. In pretending that a relationship continues to exist, long after it has had its day, we cut ourselves off from the possibility of exploring new friendships.

Job and Work Ruts

People often fall into a line of work rather than choose a course of action or career, or they remain in an unsatisfactory job because it seems too risky to change. Even the most ordinary job should offer some degree of personal satisfaction, be it no more than getting better at the work you do and receiving recognition for it. Work takes up such a large portion of our lives and is so vital to the image we have of ourselves that no one should allow it to just happen.

Place Ruts

Many people find themselves living in a town they dislike, in a neighborhood they dislike, in an apartment they dislike. Their failure to move reflects an inability to break out of a prison to which they have the exit keys. Our physical surroundings color our feelings about everything. One of your exciting potentials as an unmarried, unburdened person is that you can change your surroundings if you really wish to.

Life-Style Ruts

How routinized is your existence? Do you go from home to office to home again, pretty much on schedule, with dinner always at seven and a movie once a week on Friday night? Are you resolutely committed to a certain way of life because you believe unquestioningly that it is the only way "respectable" people lead their lives? Have you determinedly arranged your activities around what you hope others will see as a "hip" life-style? These are extremes, of course, but they do exist. The point is this: To live successfully as a single, you should take as much advantage as possible of freedom, and make your own decisions about how you lead your life. You have the opportunity to do whatever is necessary to improve your way of life as you (and only you) see fit—and these changes can range from minor adjustments to a total overhaul.

Age Ruts

On the face of it, the age rut may appear a little more hazardous where women are concerned, but the problem eventually hits both sexes with nearly equal force. From childhood until middle age, we all share that error in perspective which causes us to see life as open-ended. It often comes as a shock when we realize (around age forty or so) that time is not an unlimited resource. Some people become so stricken with regret for their "lost youth" that they suddenly give up all hope of continuing to grow.

Society offers little help in coping with such a crisis, for there is an inordinate emphasis on youth and a good deal of mythology to the effect that "you can't teach an old dog," etc. But, of course, there is no age limit on freedom or personal growth. If anything, both may be better appreciated later in life, when we know their value. Singles, particularly, are better able to resist the age rut because their ability to utilize their time, money, and concentrated energy is relatively unencumbered by commitments to things, institutions, or other people.

Status/Money Ruts

These ruts keep us working at a job from which we get little or no intrinsic satisfaction but which provides a salary and status. In any society where success (even in the arts) is defined in terms of financial reward and an important-sounding title or honor, it is terribly difficult to set one's own standards for accomplishment and to live by that standard.

Escapist and Time-Wasting Ruts

In a society that makes escapism and wasting time a high art, the only limit on possible diversions is our imagination. What makes activities escapist or time-wasting? When they are out of balance with our other activities—work, plans, or other parts of our lives. You, of course, have to be the final judge of what is useful activity to you, and what is useless. We have all been given different "consciences"—different expectations for ourselves—in these matters by parents, teachers, etc. Fortunately, we can almost always discriminate between useful and useless. Doing one thing may make us feel good; doing another leaves us with a hangover of regret. The way out of this rut (as with others) is a simple push toward what you know to be positive activity. If one had to make a general rule, it might come down to "doing is better than watching."

Negative Self-Image Ruts

We've been talking about your self-image all along. Many singles, just by virtue of being single, have a negative self-image. Singles are supposed to be irresponsible, selfish, unable to make it in the "normal" world. If you are single and you still believe that, you have a negative self-image.

Obviously, the first tactic in revamping your self-image

must be to accept in your heart the major premise that it's okay to be single. But if it were all that easy, this rut would be no problem. It takes a deliberate act of will to see yourself in a more positive light. You can begin by doing and thinking the things that you know will make you a better person and by giving up a portion of those old habits and attitudes that you know are dragging you down. This last is difficult, and it is why most of us can fall into this rut from time to time, since we don't want to question the way we lead our lives all that much. If you hear yourself saying, "What the devil, I'll never change, so why bother working at it?" then you're in a negative self-image rut.

There are plenty of other ruts, and it doesn't take a degree in psychology or a great skill at self-analysis for most people to know when they are in them.

Why don't people who see they are in a rut try to get out? Well, at the bottom of all of these ruts is yet another more basic one.

The Not-Taking-One's-Losses Rut

People don't like to admit they have made a mistake, and therefore they often go on perpetuating an error hoping it will somehow turn out all right. This is analogous to the way in which people will often hang onto a poor stock long after it has slumped in hopes it will somehow start climbing again. What they need to do in many cases is get out and "cut their losses."

Similarly, singles need to admit it when they are in the wrong job, apartment house, relationship, friendship, part of the country—whatever. It is always easier to coast along making no decisions and doing nothing. But doing nothing is doing something—and the something you are doing is by-passing all the positive benefits that can come to you once you cut your losses and go on to something better. Again, married people may more easily rationalize to themselves or each other why they cannot make a change or take a chance; you, as a single, cannot afford to do so.

FEAR OF DECISIONS

Most people hate to make decisions and will allow religion, the toss of a coin, an authority figure, family pressure, the government, events—almost anything—to determine what happens to them. Indeed, marriage itself is probably often entered into because it is one decision by which many people hope to escape ever having to make another one.

Using your freedom means making choices, deciding between alternatives, without always knowing how things will turn out. Most people fear the unknown and have a low tolerance for ambiguity—they are uncomfortable when things aren't definite and predictable. They seek security at the cost of life itself.

Accepting the inevitability of change in our lives and being comfortable with it is an essential for decision making.

Many people enter the single world through the death of a spouse or through divorce or separation. For them, a terrifying change has just taken place, and their ability to undertake others is sometimes very much curtailed. They grab for anything or anyone who offers the security they have just lost. This is understandable, and for a while, it may even be wise for them to simply absorb their experience, but they must be especially wary of fixing their lives rigidly into a pattern where they view themselves more as ex-marrieds than as singles for whom a world of new choices is now available.

People fear decisions because they are afraid to make mistakes. Although intellectually we may accept the idea that as human beings we will be wrong part of the time, emotionally we too often carry over from childhood the memory that when we made a mistake—even a trivial one like spilling the milk or not turning out the lights in our room—we were made to feel "bad," "no good," "stupid." So, instead of looking ahead to the benefits and eventual pleasures of taking a risk or making a choice, we retreat hastily back to the familiar and safe, where we are unlikely to feel such anxieties or look foolish.

The way to get beyond the emotional fear is first to recognize it for what it is—early childhood conditioning—and second, to understand and resolve to take advantage of the learning potential that is inherent in mistake making. Once we give up trying to be perfect, a "wrong" decision can turn out to be "right" if we use it as a stepping-stone to growth.

George Bernard Shaw, asked for literary advice by a young critic, once replied: "You wrote you are scarcely competent to write books just yet. That is why I recommend you to learn. If I advise you to learn to skate, you would not reply that your balance was scarcely good enough yet. A man learns to skate by staggering about making a fool of himself. Indeed, he progresses in all things by resolutely making a fool of himself."

Still another reason people fear making a decision is that it involves taking responsibility for oneself. Making decisions by oneself—and for oneself—frequently means doing things that other people may not want you to do. But the single person is blessed—and no lesser word accurately describes it—with a greater ability than a married person to pursue a life of his own.

In fact, most people would rather not make any decisions

at all if they can avoid it. They just go along with what happens. They don't choose; they react. Or they pretend that the big problems in life just don't exist: What do I want to do with my life? How do I go about it? What kind of friends do I want? Do I want a close relationship with him (or her)? Do I want to marry him (or her)? These are major questions that have to do directly with the quality of lives we lead, and in examining them, even briefly, we are forced to look at our most treasured assumptions about life and ourselves.

YOU COME FIRST

We have all grown up with a false assumption that has stunted our imagination and has led us off on tangents where our own lives are concerned. It is this: It is selfish to want to live your own life; that is, you must think of others first and yourself later. Somehow, later never comes.

When you are single, have decided to accept being single, and finally go about your business of being single and feeling good about it, there will always be someone around to remind you that you aren't being fair—to your family, society, your friends, your lover, and ultimately to yourself. Just as there is a prejudice against being single in society, there is an equal, if not greater, prejudice against being free and making the choices that will let you lead the life you want to lead. But ultimately one must face the question: For whom am I living my life? The answer, I am living it for myself, doesn't mean that you are not interested in the well-being of others and are not prepared to make reasonable sacrifices for them. What it does mean is that you are unwilling to give up your life, your goals, and your hopes to fulfill someone else's. If you try to please someone else at your own sacrifice, no one wins. You may not even know what the other person really wants, and he may not necessarily know himself.

Others may argue that if you do what you want, you will be hurting somebody else. But who will you be hurting, and why should they be hurt, after all? There is no pleasing everyone, as we all know. The truth is that when you please yourself, you usually end up pleasing other people, too, because they will sense in you your integrity and your sense of fulfillment. And that will enhance their lives and give them the stimulus to do the same.

For example, Earl, a never-married thirty-nine-year-old, discovered that in pleasing himself he was actually achieving the kind of relationships with other people he had always wanted but hadn't known how to develop. Because Earl was so likeable and generous and such a good listener, he was constantly being called on by his friends for help, advice, and companionship. Although these calls interrupted Earl's own activities, he was reluctant not to respond to everybody else's needs.

In his younger years he had not minded the interruptions so much, but as he got older, he was bothered by requests for his time coming so frequently, particularly when he became interested in designing and making wood furniture in his evening hours. Finally, he made a decision. He told all his friends that, except for an emergency, to call him only before seven o'clock or after nine-thirty at night. Suddenly, many of his friends found that their requests really weren't emergencies and could be put off until Earl could deal with them at his convenience. He was able to recapture his evenings to use for his own benefit. Earl learned that other people accept the evaluation you put upon yourself.

Phyllis had a different problem. Divorced for one year, she

lived alone in an apartment about three miles from where her widowed mother lived alone in a small house. Because her mother's health was growing poorer, it became obvious to Phyllis that sooner or later she would have to come to a decision about her mother. The alternatives: Her mother would have to move in with her, or she would have to move in with her mother, or her mother would have to move into a rest home of some sort.

Since Phyllis' work involved travel from time to time, she felt it would be difficult to live with her mother in either of their homes. Also, because it would curtail her freedom considerably, to say the least, she really didn't want to live with her mother at all. She searched the area until she finally found an attractive place for older men and women and moved her mother there. The decision wasn't easy, and it led to an enormous amount of guilt. "What a thankless daughter I am. How could I do this to my own mother? What will other people think?"—thoughts like these kept troubling her.

Under this strain, she wondered if she ought to go back on the decision, give up her job, get another which did not require travel (even though she made a fine salary and loved her work), and move her mother out of the rest home and in with her. She wrestled with the idea for three agonizing weeks before deciding to talk it over with her mother. To her surprise, her mother told her she liked being in the "guest home." In fact, she preferred it. She had companions her own age to talk to, and she had discovered several other women who shared her interests. She felt a greater sense of freedom and enjoyment where she was and admitted she did not really want to live with Phyllis. Phyllis also learned from the "confessions" the two made to each other that her mother was much more reluctant to talk about her real feelings than Phyllis realized.

Phyllis, in deciding to relocate her mother, was really exercising her freedom to act in her own behalf. While she irrationally feared some dread retribution as a result of making a decision based entirely on self-interest, it turned out she was really pleasing another by pleasing herself.

But what can you do if your elderly parent or parents do want to live with you and you don't want them to? This sometimes happens, although generally, older parents prefer living by themselves. Making a decision in this area can be one of the most difficult and even traumatic experiences any single can have.

If you have a good relationship with your parents and if your way of living, habits, likes, dislikes, etc., are somewhat similar, then a decision to live together may not be so difficult, especially if they don't interfere in your life. If, however, you are very different people, and if you feel your freedom would be so curtailed that you would feel almost imprisoned, then a firm No on your part may be necessary.

Of course some circumstances will not permit a No—illness on the part of the parents, not enough money to pay for nursing home care, no nursing care available—in which case you may have no other choice but to have your parents move in with you.

Looking at it from your standpoint, though, if you are financially able to have them cared for by any other means than having them living with you, this may be the wiser decision for all. If your parents moved in with you, or you with them, against your will and better judgment, then the amount of resentment that might build up in you could very well make living together almost intolerable. It could even lead to psychosomatic illness for all of you.

Before making such an important decision, talk it out at length with your friends, especially those who have faced a similar problem. They will be able to help, and you will stand a much better chance of making a wise decision, one that will be good not only for you but in the long run for your parents be good not only for you but for your parents too.

What Earl and Phyllis did, and what you can do, is choose positively, that is, determine which of the choices will fulfill you to the greatest degree, rather than which will give you the least discomfort. Don't worry that you are going to turn into a titan of selfishness. The built-in pressures of past training, common sense, and decency will stop you. Don't be deterred by the fact that most people spend most of their time making negative decisions—successful lives are built on positive ones.

DISCOVERING YOUR GOALS

With all the emphasis nowadays on enjoying the pleasures of the moment, it may seem a little old-fashioned to talk about goals. Why indeed have goals? Our answer is that since human beings seem to be basically purposeful, goals are a necessary part of human existence. There is plenty of evidence—old as well as new—which tells us that the happiest people are those that have found a meaning, purpose, and directions in their lives.

When we are too engulfed by everyday pursuits, when we ignore the "long view," we fail to discover or we lose the pleasure of living. Having goals gives purpose to life, contributes to this pleasure, and helps us order our priorities—in people, activities, experiences, work, time. This, in turn, helps us distinguish between what is important to us and what is not.

Sometimes an awareness of the meaning and purpose of life strikes people when they reach middle age and become concerned with the finiteness of their lives. It also happens frequently in the wake of a crisis like divorce or widowhood. We have all read stories of people reshaping their lives after a brush with death forced them to think seriously about what they wanted from life. It is unnecessary to wait for dire circumstances to wake us up to the fact that we are free, after all, to choose what we want to do with our lives, no matter what our age or circumstances.

To have a meaningful goal, one doesn't need a monumental purpose like doing some tremendous community good or creating something of value to anyone other than oneself.

To help you discover your goals, we suggest an easy do-it-yourself technique called the "Goals Inventory" that may start you seriously thinking about what you want to be doing five months from now as well as five years from now. It has worked well for many singles in "Challenge" workshops.

Pick a time when you are alone and in the mood for self-searching. If you've never thought much about your over-all goals, we recommend that you set aside a minimum of thirty minutes for this first inventory. You may find yourself becoming so intrigued with what you learn about yourself that you will spend hours on it and several more days thinking over the results.

Take out three pages of paper and on the first sheet write the heading "What I'd like to be doing five years from now." Then start writing down as fast as you can all the things that come to your mind. They may be whole sentences, phrases, or simply one word. The important thing is not to stop writing, but to let your thoughts flow freely as in the free-association technique, where one word or idea calls forth another, often from your subconscious mind.

On the second sheet of paper write the heading "What I would like to do within the next five months if I knew that was all the time I had left to live." Again, write as quickly as you can. This time, you may dredge up some very sobering thoughts about things or people you didn't even know you had. This list is apt to be shorter than the first one, as those deeper values—things very important and precious to you—push themselves into your consciousness.

Now read over both lists and see how many items are common to both. Those that appear on both sheets are likely to be the ones of greatest importance to you and the ones which you probably have the greatest motivation to pursue as life goals. If you have been as honest as possible in giving your responses, these lists will provide some real clues to the direction your life might take.

Finally, on the third sheet of paper, write: "How I can set about accomplishing these things." Once more, as fast as you can write, list things you can do, names of people who can be of help, classes, jobs, places, books, ideas—anything you can think of—that might be stepping-stones to your goals. You may find you are already on the track of what is important to you and have only to continue doing what you're doing. But in most cases it will require planning and probably even some radical changes if you are to truly pursue your goals.

Thirty-eight-year-old Karen, a never-married secretary, took this self-test for goals during one of the "Challenge" workshops and found to her surprise that she had never pursued a career because she always felt that one day she would get married and stop working. Why should she bother finding out what her talents were if all she ever told herself was, "I'm just temporary?"

After giving herself this test, she realized she had allowed herself to feel "temporary" for twenty years—ever since graduating from high school. With further self-analysis, she realized she did not have an overwhelming desire to be married at all. Armed with this rather startling but satisfying discovery about herself, she decided to go back to school in the evenings to study merchandising, which had always interested her. She is now working as an assistant buyer in a department store.

Society prescribes for all unmarried women a single, un-varying goal—marriage. Once you take away that goal or reduce it to secondary importance, it is a rare woman who will not, at times, feel rudderless. She needs to discover by careful thought that she is free to pursue other goals, free to explore a world of potentially rewarding work and relationships.

Men, trained since boyhood to aim themselves at some career, often have an opposite problem; they are so work-oriented that they fail to pursue those activities from which they receive other satisfactions.

Ted, a fifty-five-year-old newly divorced insurance agent who took the Goals Inventory, was confronted with the fact that both his immediate and long-range goals had to do with finding some way to make a living out of the one interest he had always pursued with a passion—rock collecting. He was surprised at this because he had never allowed himself the time or tranquility to even consider how he might want to spend his life. Now that his children were grown and his marriage was over, he felt he had nothing to lose except a career choice that he had grown tired of anyway.

So Ted started in a small way by polishing his stones and mounting them in rings and brooches he learned to design in a high school adult education course. Then he took them around to some boutiques and specialty shops, which took them on consignment. When they sold, he made more and got better at it. Finally, he felt secure enough to give up his regular job.

Today, a year and a half after making his decision, he has achieved the life he wants—after a lifetime of believing it was impossible. While he is not yet making nearly as much money as he once did, he's more fulfilled than ever before, and that—not the dollars which are supposed to bring happiness—is what is important to him.

DOING THE WORK YOU ENJOY

Nowhere does the single life offer more opportunity than in the area of work. Not only do singles have more freedom to move, to choose, to change, to explore work situations, and to find the work they most enjoy doing, but they have a stronger motivation to do these things well. Or they can have. Singles who enjoy their lives and their freedom almost always have a strong work commitment, too.

Since work is how we spend half our lives, it stands to reason that if we make it as useful and rewarding as possible, it is going to be an enormous source of satisfaction for us. For many people, happiness seems to be a by-product of work. Certainly for most of us—especially singles—work can help us maintain perspective in other areas of our lives, especially our love relationships. Men know how work can act as ballast, since they have long been trained to take work seriously, but many women are just beginning to discover what an enormous satisfaction serious, dedicated work can be.

It is all very well to talk about doing the work one enjoys doing. It is entirely another thing to find it. And it is another thing again to find it at a salary that you can live on comfortably. This is a problem, of course, for both sexes. But since most single women have to be self-supporting and are usually paid less than men doing the same work, the problem is especially acute for women. Economic problems tend to be most severe for divorced and widowed women of any age who have never worked at all. These realities and inequities of the marketplace needn't stop you. They haven't stopped others. What is needed is a realistic appraisal of what you are up against, the determination to find a way around these obstacles, and a plan to do so.

GETTING INTO WORK YOU ENJOY

A few lucky people, almost from early childhood, know what career they want to follow. Most of us don't. And the career decisions most of us make during our late teens and early twenties often turn out to be the wrong decisions. We can outgrow our jobs just as we do people. Today, fortunately, when people in their thirties, forties, fifties, and older, find themselves dissatisfied because the work they are doing is not fulfilling, they are finding ways to change their jobs or careers.

If you are not doing the work you want, or even if you've never worked before, the following strategies can be useful to you, depending, however, on the economic facts of your life.

But remember, whatever those economic facts, they can always be reinterpreted in a new light. Perhaps as a single you may be able to manage for awhile with less money than you are accustomed to having.

Essentially, the following strategies involve what is usually referred to as getting your foot in the door, which any seasoned job hunter will tell you is half the battle.

Apprentice Yourself

We are not advising that you work for nothing, but we are suggesting that if you show that you are enthusiastic about learning more about the job, plenty of businesses will take you on and let you learn a trade or craft if you are willing to contribute your nominal skill for a nominal salary. A fair exchange! Many singles took their first step toward becoming mechanics, buyers, designers, decorators, and craftsmen in just this way. If you decide to do this, you would do better to approach smaller companies, since large organizations have stricter hiring policies. But don't think of yourself as an apprentice forever. Expecting and asking for more money is part of developing self-esteem.

Work at Night

Particularly in metropolitan areas, a surprising number of establishments are open at night, or at least part of the night. They are often eager for night personnel, and because fewer marrieds are free to work at night the field is wide open to singles.

One widowed woman of forty-five found her first job as a library assistant during evening extension hours at a nearby university. She was so eager and industrious that she was asked to put in some time during the day. It wasn't long before she was combining part-time library work with part-time course work leading to a library degree.

A retired widowed man who had always been interested in nutrition found a job working as a clerk in a health food store primarily because he was available for the nighttime hours when they were open. On the basis of the skills he had gained in this experience, he was later able to find a full-time job managing a shop.

Work Part-Time

Being master of your own time, you, as a single, are also able to take advantage of the innumerable and rapidly growing opportunities for part-time work. Part-time work offers the advantage that you can explore an area of interest and see how you like it before committing yourself to it on a permanent basis.

One fifty-eight-year-old widowed woman who loved children, had no grandchildren of her own, and had to earn money but had never worked in a job before, found she could earn very good money managing households and children while parents were away on trips. At first she couldn't picture herself as a "sitter," thinking of it as a social comedown, but when necessity prompted her to begin working, she found it fun and rewarding, and it paid well. She was even more pleased later on when she expanded her operation to take care of five or more children in her own home, picking them up after school and keeping them until the parents returned from work.

One young never-married man of twenty-two had once worked on a neighborhood newspaper and wanted eventually to become a news reporter. In time he worked into such a job with a wire service by first taking a job answering the phone in one of its offices on Saturdays.

Create a Job

George Bernard Shaw, when asked his advice about work, replied, "The people who get on in this world are the people who go out and find the jobs they want—or if they can't find them, they make them." There is a whole, wonderful world of truly interesting jobs out there that never existed until someone saw a need and did something about it.

Jack, divorced and tired of running a menswear shop, searched his background and skills for other work he might enjoy more. A trained athlete, he realized that it might be possible to combine this avocational interest in sports with teaching, which he also thought he might enjoy. He placed an ad in a local paper offering Saturday tennis lessons. Before he knew it, he had many clients. He soon began offering swimming lessons as well and eventually was able to establish an after-school boys and girls recreation club.

A widowed woman we know, while married, had enjoyed getting all her surplus possessions together from time to time and having neighborhood garage sales. Then when her husband died, since she and her two sons were moving to a small apartment from a big house, she did it on a grand scale, selling most of her furnishings. She did so well financially and it all went so smoothly that friends, and friends of friends who were emptying their attics or moving began to call her to do a similar sales job for them. Soon she had built up a small, profitable business.

Other Techniques

Other strategies for getting into work you enjoy can be employed, too. All of them involve planning, originality and initiative—in a word, using your freedom. In some cases, singles are already doing work they essentially enjoy but they seek more desirable surroundings to do it in—or ways to combine a work goal with, say, a recreational goal.

For example, a divorced sporting-goods salesman in Chicago who enjoyed his job but wanted to live in a warmer climate wrote letters to five major department stores in Southern cities detailing his experience and offering his services. Two wrote back offering him a job. Within a month, he was happily settled in Miami enjoying his new position.

A young never-married secretary, who liked her job but wanted to travel, checked in the library and with the chamber of commerce for the names of all the firms in her city that had overseas offices. She wrote letters of application to all of them and got back several job offers. People who try this kind of realistic goal-directed planning for the first time are always surprised when they discover that knowing what you want and wanting it strongly can influence other people in your favor.

A single woman was tired of working as a bookkeeper in a grocery store and wanted more time for sports and recreation. She found what she wanted by assiduously tracking down jobs with health clubs and spas until she found a spot where her business training could be put to work while at the same time giving her extra hours to pursue her health interests.

If in spite of all your explorations you are still not sure what work you should be doing, by all means avail yourself of a good career or vocational counselor. Good counseling services are usually available on most university campuses, and these facilities are generally available to the public for a fee. Women's centers connected with many universities and colleges are particularly attuned to women's needs in the job market.

The Working Parent

As a single, you have the opportunity to take chances, especially if you are without children. But, even if you have children, the problem of changing jobs and finding the work you want to do is not insoluble. Children are movable too, and far more adaptable than we give them credit for. If the child feels reasonably secure in the parent's love, then things such as moving are not so important. Besides, if everything you do is geared to the child and not to your own well-being, you are not doing the child a favor. The child, sensing your resentment and dissatisfaction, will probably resent you, too.

As a parent, you usually know what is best, and doing what is best for you is probably best for the child in the long run. Of course, the child may not see it this way for a long time, and it may not be easy for you during the transition, but you are giving your child a first lesson in freedom by breaking the cycle of martyrdom—from parent to child—so long promoted by society.

A single working (or would-be working) parent just has to be doubly ingenious at figuring out arrangements that will do right by the children while preserving the freedom he or she wants. Sue and Valerie, two young single mothers in a "Challenge" workshop, told of sharing the cost of a joint apartment and a live-in "sitter" so that each could pursue her career, one as an executive secretary and the other as a teacher. There were problems and difficulties, of course, but they were outweighed by the pleasure of finding an alternative way to get around the frustrations of trying to be a parent and a productive person in the workaday world at the same time.

"If you asked me a year ago," said Sue, "I would have said there was no solution to my problems—my marriage was breaking up, I had two children, no money, no time for myself—doomsville. Then I said to myself, 'Darn it, I want to teach. Why should I wait twenty years till my children are grown? I want to do it now.' My friend Valerie felt the same way. We sat down and found a way. And the children seem to enjoy themselves more than they did when we were each a separate family."

Naturally, finding a work situation that combines several of your interests or goals is no guarantee that your life will be magically transformed. You may not like the new work situation, you may decide you were better off where you were, or the project may disappoint you in other ways, but the point is you are actively using your freedom to try to live the life you want.

If you don't like what you're doing, it is always easier to stay put, to do nothing. People will seldom ask you, "Why haven't you changed jobs?" but some friend or relative is almost sure to say, "I *told* you you shouldn't have done that," if you do make a change you are not too happy about. If this happens, forget it. It is far more important that you have no occasion to confront yourself with the fact that you didn't dare take a chance.

Most people still lead what Thoreau called "lives of quiet desperation"—working at jobs they don't like, living in places they don't want to live in, and staying in relationships they don't really like. You don't have to be one of them.

FREEDOM IS BEING YOURSELF

There is an old story about a "man searching the world for the secret to personal fulfillment. He crossed the deepest crevasses, trudged through deserts, crawled and hacked his way to the top of the highest mountains. Ragged and exhausted, he finally arrived at the place where he had been told the secret would be waiting for him. When he got there, he found a little box. Inside was a mirror bearing the inscription "There is no secret."

There is no secret outside ourselves. You have only to look in the mirror to realize that within yourself lies the secret. The proper use of freedom is the key to the successful life. It is probably the key to everything else in life as well—especially self-esteem—and that is what this whole book is primarily about: self-knowledge and freedom.

We have tried to help you see some of the fears, evasions, myths, illusions, compromises, untruths, and ruts that get in the way of your realizing the potential inherent in the single state. We have tried to show how these obstacles keep you from perceiving the reality of your own situation.

But recognizing where you are is only the start—acting on what you now know is the essential. As you dare to take risks and change the things about your life that you don't like, you start liking yourself more. And liking yourself more leads to self-esteem.

As you risk going out alone or taking a new job, as you really come to know what you want for yourself, as you seek significant friendships, as you confront the myths that work against you, as you choose—really choose—among alternatives, you become freer and freer. And the freer you become, the more you will like and respect yourself. And when you feel good about yourself, which is what self-esteem is all about, you can then feel at home in the world.

This freedom is something that you already possess just by virtue of being single. You just didn't know you had it.

In *The Wizard of Oz*, the Tin Woodsman, the Cowardly Lion, and the Strawman learn that they already have all that they traveled so far to ask from the Wizard—brains, courage and a heart. All the Wizard of Oz could really do for them was to make them aware that they already owned what they wanted so badly.

The challenge of being married lies in compromise, accommodation, learning to work in tandem, bringing up a family, focusing on longer-range goals, and just staying married. In trying to do all this, many marrieds find themselves trapped in dull, routine chores and treadmill obligations. The price that is often required in marriage—turning one's back on one's personal growth and freedom—is often higher than they want to pay (or the divorce rate would not be as high as it is).

We probably ought to reiterate here that we are not against marriage. But it works best when it is between two free people who are aware of alternatives and who decide they prefer to be married. So if you decide marriage is really what you're after, it becomes even more important that you learn to cultivate your sense of freedom avidly. It is one of the most important wedding presents you can give your new spouse.

The more you dig out of your ruts, the more you transform loneliness so that it works for you, the more you put the effort of the search for the one-and-only into the search for your true self, the more you discover your goals and do work you enjoy, the freer you will become. And the final freedom of all is feeling free enough to be yourself—so that you can choose with conviction the life you want to live.

When you have done this, you will probably find that other areas of your life begin to fall into place. Along with this new-found freedom you will be feeling respect, acceptance, and caring. They cost nothing, yet you cannot buy them for any price. Start today by giving them to yourself first. Then they will automatically overflow to others.

As a single, the most important present you can give yourself is the exercise of your freedom. Far from being the second-class citizen society has always said you were, you are in a position to become truly a first-class person.

Over the years that "The Challenge of Being Single" workshops have been meeting, the ideas we have been analyzing on these pages emerged as being particularly helpful and pertinent to the participants. To serve as a quick refresher when you need it, they have been drawn together and summarized in the Singles Manifesto which follows. We hope it will be a continuing stimulus and encourage you to recognize the potentials in the single state, harness them, and use them to maximum advantage.

THE SINGLES MANIFESTO

PREAMBLE: Whereas the written and spoken word about singles has been and continues to be one of gloom and doom, untruths and misinformation, we the singles of the United States—divorced, separated, widowed and never-married—in order to bury the myths, establish the truths, uplift our spirits, promote our freedom, become cognizant of our great fortune as singles, do ordain and establish this manifesto for the singles of the United States of America.

ARTICLE I

Attitude toward self:

1. As a single, I shall appreciate myself as a unique person with a special combination of traits and talents no one else has.
2. I will develop and maintain a healthy self-respect and a high sense of self-worth, knowing that I cannot respect and like others until I first appreciate myself.
3. I will at all times take responsibility for my own actions, knowing that responsibility begins within my own self.

4. I will strive to put all my talents to work so that I can eliminate any residual, socially induced feelings of inferiority, knowing that when I give of myself to others, my self-esteem will rise accordingly.

5. I will have goals, knowing I will feel a sense of elation and heightened self-esteem once the goal is accomplished.

6. I will give myself rewards when I have accomplished a goal or difficult task, knowing the more I practice the spirit of giving to myself, the more I will be able to give to others—and rewards, like charity, begin at home.

7. I will take an entirely new look at loneliness, knowing there is a vast difference between loneliness and being alone, realizing further that loneliness is a part of the human condition and that facing it when it happens will allow me to appreciate the positive side of being alone.

8. I will, in my deepest feelings, know that it's okay to be single and, becoming braver, know that it's even more than okay—it can be a great and untapped opportunity for continuous personal growth.

ARTICLE II

Attitude toward others:

1. I will stop searching for the "one-and-only," knowing that as I become more free to be myself, I will be freer to care about others, so that relationships will come to me as a natural consequence and I will feel free to accept or reject them.

2. Instead of searching for the "one-and-only," I will realize the tremendous importance of friendships and will develop understanding, worthwhile friends of both the same and opposite sex. I will realize that platonic friend-

ships are not only possible, but a necessary part of a successfully single life.

3. I will take inventory of my present "friends," by-passing those who are negative and harmful and cultivating those who are helpful and nourishing.

4. I will, when I attend singles' affairs, consider the singles I meet there as potential friends, not as "losers," knowing my attitude will color my perception even before I step in the door.

ARTICLE III

Attitude toward society:

1. I will appreciate that all four categories of singlehood—divorced, separated, widowed, and never-married—suffer similar discriminations and that we are much more alike than different, no matter what our age or sex.

2. I will appreciate that the so-called battle of the sexes is a social myth, that men and women are much more alike than different in their reaction to fear, rejection, loneliness, sorrow, joy, caring, sharing, and loving, and that, as singles, we have a unique opportunity to foster understanding and empathy between male and female.

3. I will no longer suffer in silence the injustices to me as a single, but will do everything I can to help eradicate them.

4. I will, by choosing to live a free single life, be helping to raise the status of singlehood. In doing this, I will be strengthening rather than weakening marriage, for when we truly have the option not to marry, marriage will be seen as a free choice rather than one demanded by a pairing society.

5. Finally, I will do my part in every way to promote good will between marrieds and singles, because misunderstandings will be diminished only when each of us, as a unique human being, realizes that being self-aware, autonomous, free, self-fulfilled, and whole has nothing whatsoever to do with being either married or single, but, in the final analysis, comes from being ourselves.

BIBLIOGRAPHY

Bernard, Jessie. *The Future of Marriage.* New York: World, 1972.

Browne, Harry. *How I Found Freedom in an Unfree World.* New York: Macmillan, 1973.

Ellis, Albert. *Sex without Guilt.* New York: Lyle Stuart, 1958.

———. *The Sensuous Couple.* New York: Lyle Stuart, 1973.

Fromme, Allan. *The Ability to Love.* North Hollywood, Calif.: Wilshire Book Co., 1973.

Godwin, John. *The Mating Trade.* Garden City, N.Y.: Doubleday, 1973.

Gorney, Roderic. *The Human Agenda.* New York: Simon & Schuster, 1972.

Keyes, Ralph. *We, the Lonely People.* New York: Harper and Row, 1973.

Kinsey, Alfred. *Sexual Behavior in the Human Male.* Philadelphia: W. B. Saunders, 1948.

Kinsey, Alfred. *Sexual Behavior in the Human Female.* Philadelphia: W. B. Saunders, 1953.

Klein, Carole. *The Single Parent Experience.* New York: Walker & Co., 1973.

Masters, William, and Virginia Johnson. *Human Sexual Response.* Boston: Little, Brown, 1966.

Masters, William, and Virginia Johnson. *Human Sexual Inadequacy.* Boston: Little, Brown, 1970.

Moustakas, Clark E. *Loneliness.* Englewood Cliffs, N.J.: Prentice-Hall (hardcover), Spectrum (paper), 1961.

O'Neill, Nena, and George O'Neill. *Open Marriage.* New York: M. Evans, 1972.

Rosenbaum, Jean, and Veryl Rosenbaum. *Conquering Loneliness.* New York: Hawthorn, 1973.

Shostrom, Everett. *Freedom to Be.* Englewood Cliffs, N.J.: Prentice-Hall, 1972.

Sorenson, Robert. *Adolescent Sexuality in Contemporary America.* New York: World, 1973.

SUGGESTED READING

In addition to the titles listed in the Bibliography, we recommend the following books for their helpfulness. We believe they will aid you in creating a fulfilling single life.

Careers

Encyclopedia of Careers & Vocational Guidance. Cnicago: Ferguson, 1972. Recommended for persons of any age who have never worked or who may be considering a career change.

Occupational Outlook Handbook. Washington, D.C.: Superintendent of Documents, 1972-1973. Excellent for individuals seeking information about jobs and careers.

Divorced, Separated, and Widowed

Athearn, Louise Montague. *What Every Formerly Married Woman Should Know.* New York: David McKay, 1973. Focuses on realistic and intimate questions asked by divorced and widowed women.

Bohannan, Paul. *Divorce and After.* Garden City, N.Y.: Doubleday, 1970. Emotional and social problems of divorce around the world by experts in various fields, including Margaret Mead and Jessie Bernard.

Hunt, Morton M. *The World of the Formerly Married.* New York: McGraw-Hill, 1966. A comprehensive study of thousands of formerly marrieds, covering their mores, problems, and experiences.

Krantzler, Mel. *Creative Divorce.* New York: M. Evans, 1974. A positive approach to the loneliness and daily problems of divorce. Tells how to use divorce as a springboard to growth.

Lopata, Helena Znaniecki. *Widowhood in an American City.* Cambridge, Mass.: Schenkman, 1973. An extensive study which dispels old myths and gives a sympathetic account of what widows face, who they are, and what feelings they experience.

Lyman, Howard B. *Single Again.* New York: David McKay, 1971. A practical self-help by a divorced psychologist. For men as well as women. Cover topics from dating again to in-laws to finances.

O'Brien, Patricia. *The Woman Alone.* New York: Quadrangle, 1973. Problems of single, widowed, and divorced women. Tells the author's own experiences living away from her husband and children.

Loneliness

Weiss, Robert S. *The Experience of Emotional and Social Isolation.*
Cambridge, Mass.: The MIT Press, 1973. A survey of what is known
about loneliness and what can be done to manage it.

Sexuality

Bell, Robert R. *Premarital Sex in a Changing Society.* Englewood Cliffs,
N.J.: Prentice-Hall, 1966; and Reiss, Ira L. *Premarital Sex in a Changing
Society.* New York: The Free Press, 1960. Somewhat academic but full
of interesting information, especially showing the disparity between
sexual behavior and attitudes.

Brenton, Myron. *Sex Talk.* New York: Stein & Day, 1972. A provocative discussion about communicating your sexual feelings, desires, likes,
and dislikes to another person.

Single Parent

Despert, J. Louise. *Children of Divorce.* Garden City, N.Y.: Dolphin
Doubleday, 1962. Addressed to parents who have been, or are about to
be, divorced. A compassionate book on how to help your child through
a divorce.

Gardner, Richard A. *The Boys and Girls Book about Divorce.* New
York: Science House, 1970. A warm, understanding book in which a
child psychiatrist speaks directly to children about divorce.

Travel

Fielding, Temple. *Travel Guide to Europe.* New York: Fielding-
Morrow, 1974; and Fodor, Eugene. *Fodor's Europe.* New York:
McKay, 1974. Revised yearly, these two are classics in the travel field.

Friedman, Roslyn. *Abroad on Her Own.* New York: Doubleday, 1966.
Entertaining and practical tips on how to travel alone and enjoy every
minute of it.

Self-Understanding, Self-Esteem, and
General Books

Ellis, Albert, and Robert A. Harper. *A Guide to Rational Living.*
Englewood Cliffs, N.J.: Prentice-Hall, 1961. A no-nonsense approach to
the problems of everyday living based on psychologist Ellis's rational-
emotive school of psychology.

Fromm, Erich. *The Art of Loving.* New York: Harper & Row, 1956. A classic work on understanding exactly what the title suggests—the art of loving.

Gorney, Sondra, and Claire Cox. *After Forty.* New York: Dial Press, 1973. How women can achieve fulfillment in later years. Advice on finances, work, legal rights, and sexuality.

Gustaitis, Rasa. *Tuning In.* New York: Macmillan, 1969; and Howard, Jane. *Please Touch.* New York: McGraw-Hill, 1970. Two lively first-person accounts of encounter groups. Both are good assessments and guides for those interested.

Harris, Thomas. *I'm Okay, You're Okay.* New York: Harper, 1969. A best-selling guide to transactional analysis. A positive, helpful approach toward self-understanding.

Jourard, Sidney M. *The Transparent Self.* Princeton, N.J.: Van Nostrand, 1964. Discusses the difficulties and importance of self-disclosure as a means to greater understanding between people.

Maltz, Maxwell. *Psycho-Cybernetics.* Englewood Cliffs, N.J.: Prentice-Hall, 1960. A lively how-to on using your subconscious powers. How positive thinking helped the world's most creative thinkers and can help you.

Maslow, A. H. *Motivation and Personality.* New York: Harper and Bros., 1954. Focuses on the healthy, creative personality rather than the pathological. Chapters 12 and 13 analyze how self-fulfilled people function.

Mayeroff, Milton. *On Caring.* New York: Harper & Row, 1971. Explores the meaning and importance of caring.

Missildine, Hugh. *Your Inner Child of the Past.* New York: Simon & Schuster, 1963. Leads the reader toward greater understanding of the importance of one's past in influencing one's present actions and feelings.

Rogers, Carl. *On Becoming a Person.* Boston: Houghton Mifflin, 1970. A distinguished psychologist's guide to personal growth and creativity.

Schutz, William C. *Joy: Expanding Human Awareness.* New York: Grove Press, 1967. Various techniques for becoming a better and more joyful person, based on growth-center experiences. His many other books are all helpful and recommended.

Encyclopedia of Associations. Detroit, Mich.: Gale Research Co., 1973. A listing of over 17,000 organizations in the United States. Gives location, size, objective, and other information, with addresses of each. Covers trade associations, professional societies, and fraternal, patriotic, public affairs, hobby, avocational, sports, cultural, and many other types of organizations.

HELPFUL ADDRESSES

American Association of Retired Persons
1225 Connecticut Ave., Washington, D.C. 20036
Offers temporary employment service, adult education programs, retirement preparation service to business and industry, and many other services. Publishes *Modern Maturity* (bi-monthly) and *AARP News Bulletin* (monthly).

Association for Humanistic Psychology
325 Ninth Street, San Francisco, CA 94103
Has current information on encounter groups throughout the country.

Momma
P.O. Box 5759, Santa Monica, CA 90405
A nonprofit organization offering information on how to start chapters for single parents.

Momma
P.O. Box 567, Venice, CA 90291
An irregular periodical that publishes lively, provocative, and helpful articles ($5 for 12 issues).

Parents Without Partners
7910 Woodmont Ave., Washington, D.C. 20014
An organization for single parents, both men and women. International, nonprofit, nonsectarian. Publishes a fine monthly magazine, *The Single Parent* ($5.50 a year).

The Singles Register
P.O. Box 40, Lakewood, CA 90714
A national newspaper devoted to the needs of the divorced, widowed, and never-married. Contains timely articles for and about singles, plus ads for meeting other singles. A good newspaper. We recommend it.